MINDSET FREEDOM

MINDSET FREEDOM

SEVEN STEPS TO UNLOCK YOUR POWER IN LIFE, LOVE, AND LEADERSHIP

MALITTA SEAMON
BRAD SEAMON

FOUNDERS OF INBOUND LEADERSHIP

RIVER GROVE
BOOKS

This publication is designed to provide accurate and authoritative information in regard to the subject matter covered. It is sold with the understanding that the publisher and author are not engaged in rendering legal, accounting, or other professional services. Nothing herein shall create an attorney-client relationship, and nothing herein shall constitute legal advice or a solicitation to offer legal advice. If legal advice or other expert assistance is required, the services of a competent professional should be sought.

Published by River Grove Books
Austin, TX
www.rivergrovebooks.com

Copyright © 2025 Malitta Seamon and Brad Seamon

All rights reserved.

Thank you for purchasing an authorized edition of this book and for complying with copyright law. No part of this book may be reproduced, stored in a retrieval system, or transmitted by any means, electronic, mechanical, photocopying, recording, or otherwise, without written permission from the copyright holder.

Distributed by River Grove Books

Design and composition by Greenleaf Book Group and Sheila Parr
Cover design by Greenleaf Book Group and Sheila Parr
Cover images used under license from Adobe Stock: 251501776/tonktiti, 398193336/Retouch man, 261091593/Lidiia Koval, and Shutterstock: 2119531868/Vensto

Publisher's Cataloging-in-Publication data is available.

Print ISBN: 978-1-63299-969-6

eBook ISBN: 978-1-63299-970-2

First Edition

To our parents for their love and many sacrifices.

To our sons, Brad Jr. and Chad, for their trust in us as parents and the lessons they have taught us as beautiful souls closely sharing this life with us.

To our daughter-in-love, Danielle, for embracing and strengthening our tree, and trusting us as Bibi and Baba to our grandchildren.

To our beautiful grandchildren, Parker and Kendall, and those still to come, who will give to this earth so much more than we can dream.

To our grandparents and all our ancestors, who used their lives to build ours.

To our family and friends who have listened to us talk about this book for a long time.

To each other for having the love, resilience, patience, and vulnerability to listen and learn from each other throughout this journey.

And to all of humanity: may we always remember that together we are co-creators of what we experience in life.

CONTENTS

Introduction   1

PART I: MALITTA

1: Pain to Presence   7

2: Resistance to Release   27

3: Obstacles to Observation   39

4: Victim to Valor   53

5: Ego Imbalance to Ego Consciousness   69

6: Insecurity to Inner Peace   87

7: Tip of the Iceberg to Top of the Mountain   101

PART II: BRAD

8: Pain to Presence   125

9: Resistance to Release   135

10: Obstacles to Observation   145

11: Victim to Valor   155

12: Ego Imbalance to Ego Consciousness   163

13: Insecurity to Inner Peace   175

14: Tip of the Iceberg to Top of the Mountain   185

Malitta's Epilogue   193

Brad's Epilogue   197

Appendix: PROVE IT Mindshifts Journaling Guide   201

Notes   211

Glossary   213

About the Authors   219

INTRODUCTION

MINDSET FREEDOM IS ABOUT TAKING the journey of introspection to create what is desired. We, as husband-and-wife business partners, experienced life-changing twists that triggered a series of career and personal challenges. After more than twenty years of successfully running a business together, one of us decided to walk out. That decision created an avalanche of crises that threatened our business and marriage.

In this two-part book, we share our journey through personal transformation and the lessons gained from the PROVE IT methodology of integrating external circumstances in ways that advance and don't disrupt inner peace. Our deeply personal stories demonstrate the power the mind has in creating experiences of happiness or suffering. This book opens readers to the power of shedding attachments and fear through conscious awareness and mindful living.

While *Mindset Freedom* describes our dynamics as a husband-and-wife business team, the lessons it delivers are valuable to anyone seeking greater peace and contentment. The methodology of PROVE IT represents seven steps that shifted our individual and shared mindsets and unlocked power that changed our lives forever:

P: Pain to presence

R: Resistance to release

O: Obstacles to observation

V: Victim to valor

E: Ego imbalance to ego consciousness

I: Insecurity to inner peace

T: Tip of the iceberg to top of the mountain

These mindshift lessons are shared and told from yin and yang points of view. The yin journey (Malitta's) is part I, and the yang (Brad's) is part II. It's important to remember that while yin is often associated with feminine energy and yang with masculine energy, both men and women embody qualities of both. Yin qualities include nurturing, introspection, and inward focus, while yang qualities are marked by assertiveness, expansiveness, and an outward focus. It's not accurate to link yin solely with female identities or yang solely with male identities. We encourage you to approach our story with an open mind, understanding that the lessons shared by each of us are relevant to everyone.

The best approach to engaging with this book is to focus on yourself. This inward, reflective focus is essential. As you consider the stories and lessons here, the most important person to reflect on is you. While it may seem that others in your life—such as your spouse, business partner, family, or friends—could benefit from this book, your primary attention should be on *you*! When you work on becoming the best version of yourself, your relationships in all areas of life will improve. Why? Because self-awareness, presence, vulnerability, and emotional intelligence lead to deeper, more authentic connections.

Mindset Freedom was written to prove what is possible when you make the decision to mindshift and unlock the power within you.

PART I

MALITTA

IT HAS TAKEN NEARLY HALF a century for me to embrace some very fundamental laws about life—basic laws that could have made the earlier years of my journey much less of a struggle and a lot more peaceful. But looking back, I hold gratitude for the struggles; without them, I would have so much less of an appreciation for what I now know is essential to thriving in life.

From the highs of success to the lows of failure, I have experienced the broad and slippery spectrum of realities life offers. I have been driven by natural and nurtured competitiveness, grounded by passion and empathy, but more than anything, haunted by unconscious insecurities and deeply rooted fears.

How do we undo a lifetime of well-intended but misguided pressure and directives about how we are supposed to live? How do we erase popular beliefs about success and what a *good* life should look like, after having chased them for most of a lifetime? For me, the process of erasing came in the form of a crisis I hadn't seen coming my way. If life hadn't tripped me up, making it impossible for me to stand back up as the same person I had been, I might still be living in the dark, pretending to be content with a life that demanded nothing short of self-betrayal.

My parents, grandparents, teachers, church mentors, and so many other loving and caring adults who had a hand in preparing me meant it all for my good. They gave me the same well-intended advice they'd received—life lessons that grew into cautionary tales to keep me safe, give me a better chance at having a good life, and mold me into who *they* envisioned I could (or should) be.

Their years of molding armed me with a stockpile of strategies to reap rewards and avoid pitfalls. It sounds caring and it was, but the problem is that those strategies were unconsciously built on fears. They were less about the wide range of choices I was free to make about my life and more about what might happen if I dared to step outside the safer paths known for success—their definition of success.

I followed their road map and reached a peak of that success. The fear-based strategies were lodged in my subconscious, and I unconsciously mastered what was required to avoid failure. This all worked well until that life-changing crisis landed at my door and there was no strategy in my tool kit to fix it. No one had prepared me and there had been no warning. What I encountered wasn't part of the road map or agreement for success so when it happened, I reached for the only tools I had—self-pity and pleas to the universe to make it disappear.

But it stayed. It stayed until I realized its purpose in having shown up. The crisis didn't unfold in my life because I hadn't followed the rules for surviving and succeeding. The crisis happened because I *had* followed them. The rules had locked me in a cage of "success" that wasn't big enough to hold the potential within me. My soul wanted more than the life I'd built in captivity.

Chasing the common idea of success, I routinely broke a critical universal law: Stay true to yourself. The value of "getting ahead" is something we learn so early (perhaps even subliminally) and is reinforced in nearly every endeavor right through adulthood. I adopted this value and worked to get ahead, but of course, there is never *one* to get ahead of because there is always someone ahead of the one ahead. This landed me on the same hamster wheel of life as everyone who had been pointed in this direction. We were engaged in an exhausting chase to an invisible finish line.

On the wheel, I made countless concessions and unconscious choices that required me to lie to, steal from, and cheat myself. I was not getting ahead; in fact, *I* was losing.

In desperation and under the pressure of the crisis that had shown up to teach me, I cried and asked the universe, "Why is this happening? What have I done to deserve this? Why is my life falling apart? Help me, I want to be happy." The universe responded with *prove it*! And so my journey began.

I learned to stop expecting the world to make me happy. I realized that I don't need to make sense to the world; the world needs to make sense to me. This was the start of my path to unloading a lifelong mindset that blocked what I wanted most—inner peace and happiness.

My grandmother used to tell me, "Life is meant to be a joy." I didn't understand her point of view because joy had never been my truth. Life had always seemed to be just the opposite—obligations, expectations, pressures, and uncertainty with sprinkled in moments and occasions of joy. But my PROVE IT journey opened my eyes to what she wanted me to know.

In this book, I share the life-shifting lessons I learned when circumstances forced me through a journey of rediscovery. My hope is that this book serves as a reminder to everyone who reads it to stay present in each moment, refusing to let pains from the past and fears about the future rob us of the power of a *now* mindset and consciousness. I hope my journey helps you return to honoring the inner joy you were born to know in the same way it guided me back to honoring my own.

CHAPTER 1

PAIN TO PRESENCE

> Pain: a[n] . . . unpleasant bodily sensation or complex of sensations that causes mild to severe physical discomfort and emotional distress.
> —*MERRIAM-WEBSTER DICTIONARY*

BRAD AND I MADE A bold decision to start a business together when we were in our late twenties. I call it bold because we were young parents of a toddler and an infant at the time. Brad Jr. was just two years old, and Chad was eight months. It's a stretch to describe our money situation at the time as unstable; that could imply we had something at times to make it stable.

We didn't and it was tough. But we stayed the course, struggling to outpace our mounting bills while trying to make something happen. We believed in the dream we had of creating wealth by working together in a business of our own. So we put in the grit needed to make it happen.

Over time, without realizing it, my life became an intense balancing act of long work days, an overload of commitments, and efforts to be a good mom. But I embraced it. I had been taught and I believed that everything I was doing was a normal sacrifice for success. My weekends and weekdays did not look very different. This was a *normal* requirement for success, especially for entrepreneurs. I managed to squeeze in a few hours for fun with my sons on the weekends, but even then, I was often distracted and preoccupied. I was living a lifestyle I thought was needed to create a lifestyle I dreamed of having and giving my sons.

This model of "sacrifice" molded my entrepreneurial journey and reinforced the lie I told myself that made it acceptable.

Our Launch

The decision to leave our jobs and start a business together when we had two young sons was outrageous to everyone but us. Even worse, we didn't have a specific business plan for what we were trying to create. Our simple dream was to own and run a business that we could enjoy working in together and create a level of financial freedom and security that would make us happy. It was simple and naive. But it was also the 1990s; jobs weren't so difficult to come by. We felt we had little to lose (literally). We were less concerned with what we would *do*—our attention was on the idea of what we would *be*. Many years later, I realized the significance of that nuance.

Our solution to getting the business started was to leverage Brad's background as a certified public accountant (CPA) and my experience in sales and marketing. It made sense to pitch financial services to companies that did not have in-house accounting staff. Our strategy was simple: I would pitch and Brad would perform. But after nearly seven months of falling flat using this strategy, our bills piled up. The money we had in savings was nearly depleted, and the mix of anxiety and fear we both felt was rising. Things reached a point of desperation, and we started conveniently showing up at my parents' house with our sons around dinnertime once or twice a week "just to say hi." My parents were gracious enough to ignore what was obvious. They just made sure there was always enough food for us in case we stopped by to say hello. One night after leaving my parents' house, we pulled onto our street and spotted a tow truck in front of our house. One of our car payments was behind, and we knew without speaking why the tow truck was there. We turned around and went back to my parents' house with an excuse (which I can't remember) about why we needed to leave the car in their driveway. The car stayed there until we got the money to pay what was due.

Despite our struggles and fear we kept at it, determined not to quit. We managed to get a few small client accounts and generated revenue that allowed us to cover some, but not most, of our home expenses. It became a game of rotation, paying sets of bills every other month. Looking back, I'm not sure if our resilience was motivated by confidence or pride. We had announced our decision to become entrepreneurs so loudly to so many people, despite being discouraged about our timing, that I think neither of us was willing to be proven wrong.

Eventually, our efforts led us to the federal government. We discovered its agencies that were purchasing financial services, so we redirected our focus to forge our way into government contracting. We knew that if we could ever get in, the work could create the stability we needed to grow our company. Nothing sounded sweeter than a solid foundation.

We put in a lot of work to complete the certification requirements that qualified us to work with the federal government. After getting through the process of becoming certified, we pitched our financial services to federal agencies for months and got nowhere. The agencies weren't interested in hiring a business that had no prior experience working with them. Besides, the federal government typically hired big companies for financial services—we only had the two of us. The constant rejection was beyond discouraging. We were afraid, but fortunately, we didn't talk much about our fear; we just kept trying to move forward.

In the early 1990s, the most reliable sources for marketing were the white pages and a landline phone. I diligently dialed countless federal offices every day, hoping for the slightest indication of interest. One day, we got a bite. The federal manager on the other end of the phone asked if we could provide actuaries. I assured him that we "absolutely" could. He asked me to be in his office the next day with the resumes of at least two experienced actuaries, and if they met the requirements needed, he would look into putting a contract in place with our company. My mind was racing and all I could think was, *Is this real?* I told him we would be in his office the next day with the resumes. I hung up the phone, ran across the small hall separating my office from Brad's, and asked him, "What the hell is an actuary?"

By some miracle (and the serendipity that my sister worked at a large insurance company), we got our hands on two resumes and secured our first contract. That became the pattern for our success, and we did it pretty well. Brad and I operated in a rhythm as business partners, spouses, parents, and friends.

Company Growth

Success started to flow after we got a little experience that we could leverage. The biggest challenge we faced after getting that first contract was convincing other federal decision-makers to trust us as a married partnership. Time and again, we were asked about our ability to operate objectively. "Who holds who accountable?" "Who is in charge?" "If I have a problem with one of you, then what happens?" The notion that a husband-and-wife team could hold each other accountable without disruption to the work seemed unfathomable. It was very frustrating, but it was the reality we had to accept.

Once, we put a year's worth of effort into winning a $12 million contract that we lost because the decision-maker said she couldn't trust our husband-and-wife management structure. After this loss (and lesson) we did three things. I reverted to using my maiden name, we stopped sharing our marital status, and we gave Brad the title of CEO instead of cofounder. At the time, it seemed an easier path for the man to have the top seat. I considered myself a feminist, but I was much less concerned about that than getting the work we needed to grow the business. Title and position were window dressing. Brad and I equally owned the business, so what we called ourselves didn't matter. We knew this would help our efforts, but it was surprising how much it did.

In three years, we grew the business to about $6 million in annual revenue. We started off in financial services but fell into doing conference and event planning—an easier path of opportunities for a small business to secure federal government contracts. We spent countless hours mastering the art of operations in an industry we knew nothing about, and over time, we created stand-out strategies that helped us compete and win large federal accounts to manage conferences and events across the world. We gained a respected reputation, and more doors opened. I provided oversight for operations and client experiences, and Brad provided oversight of company finances.

We created a pretty smooth cadence as a company. For years, Brad and I participated in at least one interview with every person hired to work with us. We were very intentional about building our company's culture. Again, part of our entrepreneurial vision was to enjoy the environment and the people we worked with. Things were going well. But after about five years of growth, I started having feelings of resentment. The pressure and pace required to orchestrate and deliver the company's services and sustain it felt unbalanced, and I wasn't enjoying the feeling. I was working long hours, I had a packed travel schedule, and I was still a young mother balancing homework, sports, and social activities for my sons. The arrangement of things started to bother me, and instead of appreciating Brad's contributions, I started to view him as benefitting much more than I was.

He was the important anchor of our finance area but he had a predictable and self-managed schedule, which gave him the luxury of joining business groups, taking classes, and leading the soft stuff like internal company meetings and trainings. In my eyes, he had time to invest in self-growth and got to be the good guy with staff, while I hardly had time to breathe in between client projects and was less liked because I was the one who held people accountable for performance.

By the time I started feeling resentful, we had hired a decent number of staff. The optics of the situation were problematic for me: Brad was viewed as the CEO and "owner" of the company, and I was his wife working in *his* company. The title window dressing strategy to win work had seemingly crept inside our company and was affecting personal dynamics. I felt that Brad was beginning to believe and lean into the fake hierarchy. This was a blow to my ego and my feelings. I found myself focusing more and more on the number of sacrifices I'd made, and that triggered bad emotions as I watched credit and accolades for our success flow to Brad, our "CEO."

As I allowed this mindset to take root, my rhythm with Brad began to shift. I felt he was treating me like his second-in-command. This was a hard lip bite for me, but because I wanted success (money) more than accolades, I kept trying to put up with it. But eventually, as more layers of staff were added, my resentment bubbled to the top, and it became harder for me to stuff my feelings down and pretend. Brad and I continued to share CEO responsibilities behind closed doors, so it baffled me to watch him let the misperception grow. Our arrangement had run its course with me.

From my view, I was still "sacrificing" for our success, while Brad had been able to shift into a more comfortable and much less demanding role. I was balancing C-suite duties, writing the bulk of our proposals for new work, creating work processes, and jumping in at any given time to work in the field to troubleshoot and cover whatever was needed. This might sound like a pitch for pity, and maybe it is, but I'm explaining how I saw things at the time. This had gone on for several years, and my resentment about our roles had gradually turned into anger.

By our tenth year in business, I had no interest in continuing. Brad was a great leader, and he was sitting in a seat he wanted and suited him well. He loved reading and learning about business trends and teaching our team. He had a full staff of financial professionals who needed little day-to-day involvement from him, which gave him a lot of autonomy and freedom. As I described, my reality was quite different. I didn't start the business to be Brad's employee, but that is where I landed. The pressure I was under was not the la-la land experience I'd hoped for. I wasn't jealous of Brad, but I was envious. I wanted for myself what he had. He was operating in his zone, and I was drifting further and further away from my own. I'd lost my passion and connection with the company. In the eyes of everyone, including mine, the company had become Brad's.

A Shift

I wanted out.

I was clear about my choice to leave. This was the first major hill Brad and I hit since trying to get the business off the ground. Tension and resentment spilled beyond the office into our personal life, and while my departure was not ideal, we knew we had to make a shift. The company's revenue base was solid and we were in a good place operationally, so we felt comfortable about the timing. Brad and I put together an exit plan we felt would keep the business and our marriage in a good place.

The most important part of our transition strategy was to find a good replacement for me and allow enough crossover time for me to train them. It took several months, but after an extensive search and more interviews than I can recall, we hired a COO and relocated him and his family from the Midwest. I happily dove into training him and transferring most of my responsibilities (we decided to reassign some things to other existing staff). The new COO and I worked side by side until he felt comfortable and gave me the green light I'd been waiting for: "You can go now. I've got this." I left the company. Brad and I were both happy about our decision to free me, but we were also curious to see what our new life would be like.

Well, life was nothing short of bliss. I hadn't realized how unhappy I had become working in the business. A big weight was lifted for me. I started a nonprofit to support the needs of children living in lower-income communities. I felt a sense of purpose I hadn't experienced in more than a decade. Brad and I were enjoying our home life—an added bonus was that our sons were old enough for us to have more time together as a couple. The separate lanes we created for ourselves gave us the space we needed to care about each other more than we cared about the business. I had made the right decision.

But six months into our new life, we hit a challenge. I was working in my home office when I got a call from a department director at our company. She said, "Things are getting pretty bad; I think you need to come back." I told Brad about the call and went to the office the next day. The company did not look or feel like the one Brad and I had built. I didn't know that major issues were happening in the business but quickly found out we were at risk of losing some of our largest clients, and the anxiety about the issues was causing internal conflicts and friction. The COO hire was not what we had hoped for.

Brad had hinted about problems here and there, but I think he couldn't bring himself to disrupt my new happy space with any more than the hints. But also, Brad wasn't fully aware of the damage either—he (we) trusted the COO and had given the COO the autonomy we all wanted. By the time we reached the point of the director calling me, clients were already dissatisfied and the culture in the company had taken a hit. Brad and I both knew what needed to happen.

I shut down my nonprofit and returned to the company.

Returning

Brad and I settled back into our routine as business partners, but our brief time apart seemingly had given us a better appreciation for each other. We didn't discuss what caused me to leave when we made the decision that I should return, so we didn't address how to change our work dynamic for a better partnership. But I think we were both more sensitive to the fact that we needed each other to keep the business running and growing. I felt Brad toning down the perception of hierarchy between us and heard him more frequently refer to me as his business partner. And I'd had enough space to work through my emotions and get over resentments, which allowed me to operate in a better head space and be a better partner. We transitioned rather easily into a familiar but slightly new rhythm.

By the end of that year, Brad and I had reversed the downward trend and increased the company's rate of growth beyond our projections. We were thriving and continued to compete and win. The dynamics of our partnership were not the sole reason for our success (we had a lot of great talent and energy in our company), but it was a major factor.

The growth and intensity of our projects kept me engaged for a while, but eventually, I started getting that empty feeling again. I just couldn't connect with what I was required to get up and do every day—I had no passion for it. Brad, on the other hand, loved it and seemed content working nearly seven days a week. One Saturday morning, during our car ride to the office, it struck me. There were only two reasons I was pushing myself to stay: the business made Brad happy, and the money made us both happy. I was living on autopilot, subconsciously giving priority to those two truths. As I said, Brad and I didn't discuss what drove me out of the business, so we never discussed what could keep me in it. The business was growing exponentially, but I wasn't.

Still, I stayed, and three years quickly passed. In that third year, the company faced an unexpected and major hurdle. In short, the federal government, our largest client, has contract award limitations that are based on company revenue and size. We had grown our business so rapidly and successfully that we hit our industry's revenue size limitation before we had planned and faced being ineligible to compete to keep some of our most valued contracts. We found ourselves on the verge of a serious revenue cliff, and we had to figure out how to replace about $20 million in revenue in eighteen months. It was daunting, but Brad and I created a strategy and positioned our resources to implement it. We felt confident about moving the company forward despite the hurdle we faced, and we were in it together—or so I thought.

Getting Blindsided

On October 12, 2010, around 2 p.m., I sat at my office desk, typing an email. Brad walked in and stood in my doorway. "I'm leaving," he said.

I thought it was a little early to leave the office, but I was more than happy to shut down early. "Okay, well I need about twenty minutes, and I should be good to leave." We had driven to work together that day.

His face tightened. "No, I am *leaving*." When he saw that I was about to give the same response, he added, "I'm leaving the company."

"What?" I asked, confused. I struggled to process his words and my emotions at the same time.

"I'm taking the job," he announced, as if we were just work colleagues. Now my face tightened and my adrenaline spiked.

Brad had been approached by an elected official to take a local appointment as second-in-command in the county we lived in. The two of us had discussed the subject briefly a couple of times after he was approached, but given the critical state of the business and our need to replace $20 million in less than two years, we agreed that the idea of taking the position was ridiculous and could cause catastrophic consequences for the business. We didn't have the luxury of time and could not afford the distraction. So to say I was completely shocked and blindsided by Brad's decision and attitude is an understatement.

"Brad, this is ridiculous," I said. "You know there is no way we can do this right now."

"My decision is made." He was irritated, as if he had expected me to be okay.

My head was spinning. "Your decision is made?" I could feel my adrenaline kick into a new gear. "Brad, how in the world can you stand here and say this to me? We can't—"

He cut me off, and our discussion became a loud exchange right there in my office. In all the years we'd worked together, we'd never argued within earshot of anyone, and we'd never treated each other so callously, but in that moment the gloves were off.

I started to panic as I realized I was not going to get through to him. Brad was leaving. As this thought settled in and we continued to argue, I felt a lot of things but the biggest emotion consuming me was fear. There were so many balls in the air for the business, and we couldn't afford for any to hit the ground. I couldn't wrap my mind around what was happening, and I said everything I could think to say, but nothing was moving him. I felt enraged, dismissed, and screwed.

For the next several weeks, there was angry silence and heavy tension between us. We managed to have just enough civility to discuss and make plans for his transition. I had been left with no choice; the best I could do for myself, and the company, was to put things in place as quickly as possible. What was most important was to hire an experienced CFO. Brad agreed an exit would only work after finding and training his replacement. Having learned from our failed attempt at hiring a COO to replace me, we decided that Brad and the new CFO would work together for at least two months, after which Brad would meet with the CFO twice a month and continue to participate in monthly executive team meetings. Doing this was going to allow us to keep our finger on the pulse of his replacement's progress. But above all other things we put in place, Brad committed that he would return to the company if I ever needed him to.

This was our workable solution, and while I was far from thrilled about the situation, it felt doable.

Three weeks after agreeing on a plan for Brad's exit and getting to a space where we could have calm conversations and civil exchanges about it, Brad came to my office. This time, he told me he needed to leave the company immediately and wouldn't be able to wait for us to hire the CFO. His words were, "*They* really need me. I can't let *them* down."

Sure enough, by the end of the next week, Brad was gone. I was left in the business with nothing more from him than a file of recent financial reports and a list of passwords. I had no CFO, no one to train a new CFO, and no viable prospects. Things were bad, but I didn't yet know just how bad.

The Big Threat

The business's trajectory was shaky. Time was elapsing, and our leadership structure was fractured. Part of the revenue replacement strategy Brad and I had developed was to launch new service lines. He was designated to lead that area. When Brad left, we were integrating new people, developing new operations, marketing for new clients, and handling new challenges. I had to step in to keep that moving.

On top of trying to hold new and old service operations together, I was under extreme pressure to manage the company's cash demands. Without a CFO, I had to oversee our finances. We had more than 140 employees, more than 60 consultants, multiple subcontractor partnerships, out-of-state offices and operations, and countless vendors. It was a lot, and while we were working our plan to transition away from the conference and event work, we still had those contracts, and they required large upfront payments to secure venues and equipment that were not favorable for cash flow. Often, we had millions due in deposits and prepayments that would not be reimbursed by clients for months at a time. Without a CFO and timely financial projections, I was treading deep water.

I hardly had the time to search for Brad's replacement. And because I had so little time, the process for hiring was compromised, resulting in several failed attempts to successfully bring someone on board. Twice I hired, and twice I failed. No one seemed to be able to jump in and move as quickly and competently as I needed. I knew our inability to provide adequate training was the issue, but I didn't have a solution. (Brad did not return to train them like we had agreed.)

I could feel we were starting to lose, and this only compounded what I was feeling inside. I had the title of CEO, but I was doing very little leading. Instead, I was running behind the bus, trying not to get too far behind. The goal became to just get through my days. Fear, frustration, and an entirely new level of resentment were the anchors of my thoughts and emotions, so everything looked and felt like a problem.

A mentor of mine says that every thought is a vibration, and we attract what we vibrate. Imagine an athlete stepping into an arena with a mindset fixed on everything that is wrong or everything that could go wrong. The minute that athlete makes a first move, something likely will not go well. I was that athlete. I'd spiraled into a mindset of negativity, so I didn't just hit one wall—I hit many. I was supposed to be the leader, and I had become my own worst employee.

I was supposed to be the leader, and I had become my own worst employee.

I was angry and disgruntled. My two reasons for being in the company no longer existed. Brad was gone, and the money was now more of a headache than a source of happiness. My efforts to hold everything together were only creating more discontent as I found myself working longer and longer hours.

I managed to make strides in shifting the business into new streams of revenue, but as I did this under the pressure of time, I fell prey to a series of bad decisions. Hiring in haste, several wrong people were placed in roles and given authority they should not have had, which meant I allowed good money to be used to poorly execute strategies. I was so focused on crafting plans that I failed to timely measure impact. I knew better, but even experienced swimmers can drown if they panic.

Becoming Present and Aware About Purpose

If we resist the nudges we get in life too long, those nudges will become kicks and those kicks (if we ignore them, too) can lead to crises. I was so busy running around putting out fires and being angry about having to do it that I missed some important cues—the ones coming from the true source of my pain. I was blaming my frustration on my obligations and the heavy lift that was needed to avoid the revenue cliff for the business but the enormity of my to-do list was not the problem. My to-do list was a distraction; having it made it easier to bury myself instead of facing what was happening on a more honest level. I'd settled into a practice of being comfortable in my discomfort. That practice gave me permission to stay angry, solicit sympathy, and lean on excuses for the chaos around me. It made it okay for me to stay in my emotions (my pain), and it protected me from having to look at my own choices (my power). Despite the many external and internal cues (sleepless nights, pendulum appetite swings, and constant tension), I kept pushing my way through a miserable way of life, telling myself it was simply what I had to do.

I thought burying myself and checking off important items on my to-do list would eventually land me in a better place—a more desirable normal. As if running faster and harder down the same road was going to get me where I wanted to be. What was I thinking!

Worry and struggle had become my companions. I went to bed and woke up with them every day. Nothing in my life was certain. Within a very short time, my business, finances, and marriage had all landed on shaky ground. I started to do what many do—I questioned God and begged the universe for mercy. It felt like too much to handle, and I was consumed by an endless list of "why" questions. Why was everything falling apart, why was I in such a mess, and why was I alone in feeling responsible for cleaning it all up?

One morning, I watched Brad get dressed for his job. He could not have looked any happier. I couldn't help feeling like my misery was payment for his joy. It took a lot of self-control to not walk over and simply choke him. I felt rage, but thankfully, that morning, I kept it to myself. When Brad left the house, I dragged myself to a space I had cleared as my prayer room. This is the room I used every morning to fuss at God for answers about why these things were happening and then beg for a miracle path to quickly move me out of my situation.

The rage I felt as I watched Brad dress and leave that morning drove me to seek a deeper answer. I had reached a breaking point and felt desperate for help. After fussing and praying, I plopped down in my big chair and grabbed my journal. As I flipped the pages, I ran across words I had written down after studying the teachings of Neale Donald Walsch. The words were "Asking why something is happening is a useless question that often only intensifies our perplexity. Instead, focus on an answer for 'what.' What do I choose to do?" I had been fussing and begging for an answer to the wrong question. The answer to the question "why" was never going to fix anything.

In fact, my focus on the why was a disempowering form of self-pity that I justified by telling myself I had no choice. I was consumed by the fact that Brad left me in a terrible set of circumstances "beyond my control," and so that was my mindset. The moment I asked myself what I chose to do about the circumstances, I shifted the power from outside to inside me.

In that instant, I got it.

When I was blindsided by Brad's decision to leave the company, I responded unconsciously (in reaction mode)—I immediately jumped into fight or flight. I felt a threat to my security. All that had mattered to me until I read those words in my journal that morning were my fears and disappointment. I hadn't allowed anything to penetrate through my pain. Everything I had done and read up until that point were things to justify me, not redirect me. Fear-filled thoughts and hurt feelings had hijacked my mind, and my anger was in control.

In a fear mindset, I reacted instead of responding. I jumped in to save what I *thought* needed to be saved without pausing to consider if I even wanted to save it. I did this because I didn't want my life to change, but it already had; I just hadn't accepted it. I was foolishly fighting a useless war.

This was my first major mindshift moment. I had to get present and conscious about what was happening.

I resisted the truth about Brad's decision: He did not want to be in the business, not even with me. Not accepting this only intensified the agony I felt. His purpose had shifted away from the business we had built and from me as his business partner. I was feeling sorry for myself and basking in my fears about all the changes and possible failure—all wasted energy. That energy was incapable of producing anything to help my situation and instead produced distractions that delayed me from facing inevitable truths. All my attempts to resist and repackage my circumstances and seek answers to "why" weren't going to change anything. I thought I was fighting back, but I was fighting reality. I chose the fight that was easier to accept. Life had changed, and I needed to change, too.

I read once that some of us sit in imaginary jails that have imaginary doors, complaining about how bad things are. Nothing could have been truer for me. I was responsible for every choice that landed me in jail, just as I was responsible for every choice that would get me out. I could not control Brad, and I could not control the government, but I could control how I chose to respond to them. I'd been behaving as though I didn't have a choice, and I justified this mindset by believing I was a victim. I really, really believed this.

I told myself I was doing the right thing to protect my family's security and to honor the people in the company who believed in us. I placed this superwoman cape on myself. I cloaked myself in this martyrdom and expected recognition and appreciation for it. I waited. It was never going to arrive because the truth under the cloak was that I was attempting to protect the familiar, lucrative, and cozy life my prior reality had given me. I hadn't been thrilled about not feeling purposeful in that reality, but I was perfectly willing to stick with it rather than let it go. I started to see that my anger with Brad was as much about him disrupting my comfort as it was about him betraying my trust. After this realization, I had to look at myself.

My pursuit of purpose and my presence (how I was showing up) were out of alignment. There was no unified direction within me and therefore no unified direction through or surrounding me. This put me, and the company, through an unnecessary season of suffering. Operating unconsciously and on autopilot, I was consumed with protecting against my fears about the future. The result was an emotional state that tethered me to what had been. This didn't benefit me, the business, or my marriage.

What do I choose to do?

One of the things I love about this question is that it represents a declaration of acceptance. *Why* is a form of resistance, but *what* gives me a feeling of empowerment—asserting that I am ready to move on. The faster we can rewire our thoughts to focus on our power (choice) instead of our pain, the faster we can move through any challenge. The companion to choice is contentment. Contentment is an inside job. It starts with our thoughts, but it blossoms or dies as we create narratives about our experiences.

Life was inviting me to detach from my pain, get present about my choices, and lean into my purpose as I was living through my experience. Remaining attached to what had been was an unintentional decision to suffer. When I stopped asking the wrong question (why) and shifted my thoughts to the right one (what), I empowered myself to take better action and end misery in the process. This was a major step for me (but the days ahead put this new mindset to the test).

What, Malitta, is your purpose? This was the question I had to answer to move myself out of my imaginary jail. The next several chapters walk you through my experience of becoming conscious as I worked to get clear on the answer.

PROVE IT LESSON

The more you prolong facing what your external and internal cues are showing you, the more difficult the shift in the right direction can become. Use your power of choice to make conscious (not autopilot) decisions to create the experiences desired. And remember, the only real truth is what is true in the present moment (not from the past and not imagined).

PROVE IT QUESTIONS

- What areas of my life cause me emotional pain or discomfort?
- In what areas am I telling myself, "I have no choice" or "What else am I supposed to do"?
- What is it about these situations that creates no choice?
- Am I allowing old thoughts about these situations to rob me of new and creative possibilities in present circumstances?

PROVE IT MINDFUL PRACTICES

Listen to your discomfort. Write it down, honor it, and don't dismiss or stifle it. Identify what is at the root of your pain points, and answer the question: What do I choose to do about this? Write down what is within your power today to shift to a better experience. Here are some examples:

- If finances cause consistent stress, sit in quiet and get honest about how well the structure of your commitments aligns with the flow of your resources. What commitments do not have to exist? Are you unwilling or afraid to release them? What do you choose to do about it?

- If you consistently feel anxiety and discomfort when interacting with someone, sit in quiet and get honest about what creates the "rub" causing discomfort. Is it because you aren't or can't be honest with them? Is it because you are holding an opinion or judgment from a past experience? What do you choose to do to change what you experience?

- If you feel a sense of dread about your work or obligations, sit in quiet and get honest about why you continue. Is it because it is more convenient to continue than to change to something new? Do you allow yourself to seriously explore other possibilities? Assuming you do have choices, what do you choose to do about it?

For the comprehensive PROVE IT Mindshifts Journaling Guide, please refer to the appendix.

CHAPTER 2

RESISTANCE TO RELEASE

The intensity of the pain depends on the degree of resistance to the present moment.
—ECKHART TOLLE, *THE POWER OF NOW*

Resisting Change and the Comforts of a Pity Party

Making the question "What do I choose?" my new mindset took a lot of conscious effort. It might *sound* simple, but choosing not to look outside myself during moments of extreme frustration and anger is not always easy. And making the decision to ask the question is one thing, but the journey after asking is entirely different. I didn't want to let Brad (or God) off the hook by owning responsibility for my situation. I thought Brad was selfish, and life was unfair, period. I didn't feel I deserved what I got.

So throwing a good pity party was my thing. I had plenty of good reason and was willing to invite anyone to join in as long as they could relate to (and reinforce) my mindset of injustice. But I really didn't need anyone else. I was also good at pity partying all by myself. I would soothe myself with all sorts of thoughts about what was happening *to* me. I couldn't see at the time that the more I pity partied, the more I gave life to my feelings of frustration and anger. And of course, this meant all the things that were happening out of alignment with what I wanted seemed to get worse. I was tethered to *one* outcome I had envisioned for my marriage, my partnership with Brad, and the business. And as long as I looked for that one vision, I invited and basked in more disappointment.

Even as I worked to shift my thinking, my unconscious mind continued to produce recurring scenarios. I found myself bringing up the same conversations with Brad—"How could you have done this? You're selfish. I can't believe this is who you are." My posture in the office was also often the same—attempting to tweak and reengineer rather than dismantle and rebuild.

"Old keys don't unlock new doors" wasn't something I wanted to hear—I had too much to do. I had accepted needing to reorganize, but I needed to rebuild, and that is what I was resisting. The company structure needed a fresh solution. The strategy Brad and I had crafted to shift the business and avoid the revenue cliff was not going to work because there was not going to be a Brad and Malitta duo. As a duo, we had the advantage of knowing each other in ways someone new could never fully master. I knew I needed a new set of keys (a new strategy), but sometimes what we know and what we do have nothing in common. Some employees (mostly those who had been with the company the longest) pledged their commitment to doing whatever was needed to help the company transition. Their loyalty actually added stress. Most of them were conference and event staff assigned to the work that was part of the cliff. Meaning, my most loyal staff were the ones at greatest risk. So guess what I did? I tried delaying the inevitable by giving them the green light to take on new, shorter-term conference projects that could fit within the window of time we had left. This created false hope and dug a deeper hole for me to climb out of.

Sometimes what we know and what we do have nothing in common.

Who I needed to be and what the business needed to become was never going to happen as long as I allowed the old vision of who and what we had been to live. My resistance (desire for what was quickest, safest, and most familiar) during the season we were in took me down unproductive and costly rabbit holes. A glaring bad practice was reassigning tenured staff (conference and event staff) and trying to force fit them on teams for other projects (technology projects). The result was almost always conflict, compromised quality, a breakdown in synergy, and a negative team culture. It's amazing how I could look squarely at my situation, know best practices, and still do what felt easiest. None of this was about intelligence—it was about the fears I had about everything happening at once.

My attachment to having something (whether it had diminishing value or not) gave me immediate emotional gratification. It was a bird in my hand giving me the return I wanted, and while it held no value on the other side of the cliff, I had it and it was soothing! I used the pile of obligations on my desk to hide behind.

But for my company to survive the tsunami of threats it faced, I had to release safety (the people, systems, and operations we had mastered) so I could align the right resources to build something new. I had to make sure I and the company were unencumbered by what had been. My company did not have endless resources, and time was running out.

The company's future was in communications and technology and there was little (and nearly no lucrative) synergy between the majority of our roster of existing clients and the roster we needed. In many ways, I needed to look at it as starting the business over again, but I did everything I could to try and repackage what we had. I looked at pivoting our conference knowledge and experience into private industry, but the margins were simply too thin and the terms of the contracts too unstable. I looked at becoming a subcontractor to larger federal contractor companies in need of conference services, but the span of work available was not sufficient to make it worth the engagements. Letting go of our entire conference operations in order to redirect our energy and resources to create a new company was unavoidable.

Eventually I got to what we know—sometimes we just have to rip the Band-Aid off. Time and fading options forced me to really look at what I was spending to save something I'd essentially already lost. I had no one to bounce my thoughts and ideas around with. I was afraid of spooking my executive team (they operated more like soldiers than commanders when it came to dealing with our cliff). Brad was disinterested, so he, too, was not an option. So I kept much of the discussion going in my own head as long as I could.

There is a saying that worry is like a rocking chair: It's always in motion and keeps you busy but never actually gets you anywhere. I worried day and night, and while I was doing that, like a rocking chair, I wasn't moving forward. I became an expert firefighter, responding to challenges that, intellectually, I knew to prevent by moving forward with the more difficult plan, but instead, I stayed engaged in a ground fight against erupting fires. This left my CEO station (where I should have been fighting our war) abandoned. Unconsciously, the fires were a convenient distraction.

One of my mentors often said, "Life will always show you the direction forward, and if you ignore the hints toward that direction long enough, eventually a two-by-four experience will come along to knock you in the head hard enough that you won't be able to ignore it."

Thursday, July 12, 2012

With all the angst I had about revenue continuity and client stability, I was beyond elated to receive an award notification that renewed a long-standing contract worth $17 million for another three years. This contract was outside the conference and events industry. I expected the award, but there was nothing like actually having it in hand. Beyond the obvious financial relief, this was going to be an overall morale boost for staff. So I quickly executed and returned the contract. We'd won recognition awards for the work we had done with this client, and I felt connected to the client's mission and impact. The relationship between this client and our company was solid and mutually enjoyable, but this, too, was about to change.

The day after getting the award notice that our contract had been renewed (oddly, on Friday the thirteenth), I received a request to meet with the client the next Monday. I assumed the meeting was to discuss program goals and to kick off plans for the new contract—nothing unusual. Early that next Monday, my senior director and I walked down the hall toward the client's conference room. I could feel something was off (the body never lies). My stomach felt uneasy, and I felt anxious.

When I walked into the conference room, the usual air of warmth was missing. There were no friendly greetings; in fact, the energy in the room was cold and distant. There were six or seven faces I'd never seen before squeezed in between two faces I knew very well. The conference table was too small for the solemn group gathered around it, and my anxious feelings rose to a sense of danger. My director and I had walked into some type of ambush.

Before our butts could hit the two seats saved for us, the person sitting at the head of the table began to speak. She mumbled a brief introduction of herself that I didn't quite catch but I understood from what she said that she was the top authority in the room. The next thing I heard her say, and understood, was that our services on the contract were no longer needed. She spoke so quickly and my mind raced in so many directions that I didn't catch much more of her delivery. I did process the words "discontinued and effective immediately." I would learn later that in between the time of selecting us to receive the award and the notification paperwork getting completed, a new leadership team had been brought in to run the entire agency. This new leadership team made the decision to rescind our contract and hire in-house staff to perform the work we'd been doing but their decision and our notification crossed in timing. They sat around the table postured for a controversial exchange with us as evidenced by the presence of a couple of federal agency lawyers and their chief of contracts.

The shock of the entire experience made it difficult for me to absorb everything in real time. There was no apology offered, no offer to answer any questions from us or listen to our input, and no empathy. It was clear that our company was of no concern beyond getting this meeting over with. All indicators pointed to "please just leave."

As the new director finished her brief message that they were within their right to end the contract, the two familiar faces in the room—who we'd worked with so closely—kept their heads down. I sensed they wanted to shrink and disappear, almost as much as I did, and I could sense they had been invited to give input about as much as we were being invited in the moment.

The universe had sent me a contract—a sign of hope and reassurance—that dissipated in a matter of minutes. I sat in that chair unable to hide my feelings of defeat. My head dropped, and my hands were a bit shaky. I was devastated and speechless, but more than anything, I felt overwhelming hopelessness. For some reason, this felt like the last string of hope; it filled me with thoughts that maybe I wasn't going to be able to stop everything from unraveling. The two-by-four that my mentor had warned me about had arrived.

I don't remember saying anything in that meeting. I walked back to my car and drove straight home. I couldn't face anyone or anything at my office. It was about 10:30 a.m., and I just wanted to crawl back into bed.

Scary thoughts hijacked my mind—*How am I going to announce layoffs in the middle of everything else going on, especially after announcing and celebrating the award with the team just a couple of days prior? How will I make up for the healthy profit margin I'd already factored in as part of the rebuild, recover, and reset strategy? What will people think of me as a leader when it looks like everything is falling apart?* My fear escalated to a state of terror. I was no longer having bad thoughts; I was haunted by them.

I tried calling Brad on the way home, but he didn't pick up. He was the only person who would understand. I needed him. I tried again several times after getting home but never reached him. An entire day had gone by, and I had been alone with terrorizing thoughts and fears. When Brad finally got home that evening, I ran to him and broke down. Ordinarily, my many unanswered calls would have been the first order of discussion, but I was desperate and in such a low place that it didn't matter. I needed support; I needed him. I let all of my tears and distress tumble out. I was broken.

Crying, I told Brad everything that happened in the meeting as I also screamed at God in anger about losing the contract. I told Brad they weren't giving us any runway—that things were ending with that client immediately—which meant we would have to do a layoff for the first time in the history of the company. I'd never been a crier; this breakdown was uncharacteristic for me, but I was mentally, physically, and emotionally exhausted. I needed Brad, my husband and my business partner, back.

Brad listened to me, looked at me with no emotion, and casually said, "You'll figure this out." Then he turned around and left the house. Brad walked out the door, telling me as he was leaving that he was meeting up with his team from work at a restaurant to celebrate some legislative victory they had won.

I sat there for several minutes looking at the door—empty, in disbelief, and numb. Then, I made my way back to my bed and cried myself to sleep.

Releasing

I tossed most of the night, remembering Brad coming in late but choosing to keep my eyes shut out of fear of exploding. I simply could not add another argument to my plate of stress. By the next morning, I'd somehow accepted that the only person available for me to rely on was myself, and the only thing I could do was accept what I was facing. The choice was clear: I could lean into the situation and take action or suffer through it by being angry and seeking pity. I talked to myself that morning. I wanted to move out of my mindset of weakness—thinking about what had been done to me. I knew that mindset well and understood that it had nothing to offer to the situation but more pain and distress. I remember looking in the mirror and saying, "Malitta, it is what it is—get your s*** together." Brad's dismissive attitude and indifference toward me and the situation was the slap I needed. It pissed me off enough to realize that no one was coming to save me. Had Brad consoled me, I would have made the mistake of placing hope in him again and never would have turned to myself.

I pushed myself to answer the most important question: What do I choose to do?

As I thought about things, I realized it had been a blessing that I'd been blindsided in the meeting with the client. Any heads-up about the contract termination would have certainly launched me into a fight posture and likely resulted in a confrontational exchange. Instead, thankfully, I had been left speechless. I like to think that silence was a small gift the universe gave me as it also delivered this tough-love lesson. I needed to pause and after sleeping (well, actually not sleeping) on it, I was able to consciously sit with my thoughts and separate facts from emotions.

I wanted to get to the office early so I could call the new director. For some reason calling her from my office felt more empowering, and I needed to feel in control. I didn't get her, of course, but I told her assistant I needed to schedule a follow-up meeting, and I asked that it include only the director and me. I wasn't confident I would get the meeting, let alone a meeting with just the two of us, but to my surprise, within a day or two, the meeting was scheduled. When I walked into the director's office the first thing I felt was relief. Being in her personal space set a tone that was very different from our first encounter. I was prepared to dislike her. I wanted to dislike her—I felt I deserved to dislike her—but when she greeted me and shook my hand with both of hers, I felt a warmer connection. Within minutes of speaking with her and soaking in a bit of her life through the family pictures she had all around her office, it struck me that maybe she had been about as uncomfortable as I had during our first meeting. That would explain the cold energy I'd felt. Perhaps she was just trying to get through something very uncomfortable. I could certainly relate. I was about to have that exact same experience with my own team.

I had prepared for this meeting by arming myself with outcome data, performance reviews, financial justifications, and detailed selling points about what they would lose by abruptly removing us from the project. I laid out my case and ended by sharing how I appreciated the position she was in and the need to reduce costs (an appreciation I did not have when I arrived at her office) and then asking in the spirit of collaboration if she would extend our contract for one full final year.

She listened without interrupting me. After I finished, we pleasantly shared differing points of view. It was a good meeting. She told me she would consider my request. Within a few days, she called. I had not convinced her to keep us on for a full year, but she agreed to allow the contract to continue for another six months. I considered that a win.

Surrendering is not the same as giving up. When I surrendered to what was happening, I made the decision to be at peace with releasing what would no longer serve my or the company's future. That contract, as valuable as it was to me at the time, had run its course. Its existence would have generated needed revenue, but its multiyear existence would have also kept me rooted in the past—distracting my attention and lessening the urgency to focus on more promising, longer-term priorities. Also, I didn't need to invest too much time and resources in trying to prolong an inevitable transition. Six months was a good runway.

There is a saying that the windshield on a car is bigger than the rearview mirror because where you are headed is so much larger than what you leave behind. During the remaining six months of the contract, we gained more than just revenues and profit. The transition strategy we put into place included an out-placement program to help the team that was going to be laid off find new employment. At the end of the six months, more than 90 percent of that project team had landed new jobs. The experience turned out to be a morale boost for the company. It restored a level of trust and reintroduced caring culture practices the company had been built on.

For the first time since Brad's departure, I felt like I had achieved something that mattered. I'd found my way back to *myself* and fortunately, shifted my focus away from my own crisis to what could have become a crisis for everyone else. When I released the contract and accepted it would end, I was able to take back a degree of control. The contract ended, and I had been given the grace I asked for. I walked away enlightened about the power of releasing what has served its purpose and time. This was my $17 million two-by-four lesson, and it was worth every penny.

PROVE IT LESSON

There is a difference between giving up and surrendering. Surrendering is a conscious choice that is easiest made with an optimistic mindset. Giving up can be a hopeless response easiest made in a helpless mindset.

PROVE IT QUESTIONS

- Is there something I want to let go of but am afraid to do it?
- What is it about releasing it that makes me afraid?

- What are my new possibilities if I do let go?
- Is the promise of what is possible if I free myself from it more valuable than the attachment that has me holding on to it?

PROVE IT MINDFUL PRACTICES

Grab your journal (or device). Sit in quiet for five minutes, giving attention to the thoughts that occupy your mind. Record the thoughts that cause worry, stress, or uneasiness. After you have written these thoughts down, allow yourself to imagine releasing the source of them from your life. What would that take? Write that down, decide if the timing is right (not based on your emotions but on facts), and then write down doable steps to move toward releasing what you have decided is no longer serving you.

For the comprehensive PROVE IT Mindshifts Journaling Guide, please refer to the appendix.

CHAPTER 3

OBSTACLES TO OBSERVATION

*To acquire knowledge, one must study; but
to acquire wisdom, one must observe.*
—MARILYN VOS SAVANT, QUOTED IN SANDRA FORD WALSTON,
COURAGE: THE HEART AND SPIRIT OF EVERY WOMAN

I CHAMPIONED THROUGH THE $17 MILLION contract termination, but an endless parade of obstacles continued to come my way. I worked on releasing my vice grip on the past, but because it was the only sense of security I had at the time, that process was a struggle. I had teams of leaders, and the company was still bustling with activity as we worked to pivot, but still I felt like no one understood that, for me, letting go was much more than maneuvering business priorities. I was being forced to redefine the life I'd envisioned and had worked so hard to create. I was unsure about everything, which means my pride, my sense of identity, and what I had latched onto as my purpose all suffered. It felt like finding the courage to leave someone I knew I should no longer be with but who I still loved. Another wise piece of advice I had been given is that courage is not the absence of fear but the ability to move forward in the presence of it. I admit, I wasn't feeling very courageous, and I didn't want to be.

Facing Fears

It was one thing to have to react to external circumstances that forced me to move—those events (like the $17 million contract loss) were actually beyond my control. But to voluntarily dismantle the company's infrastructure (and my personal source of security) so I could better align our resources for future success? I was more than averse, despite being fully aware that the industry changes unfolding would soon outpace my company's response if I didn't make more timely moves.

I was getting backed into a corner and had to stop the distraction game and disengage from the firefighter posture my team had become used to. I started isolating myself more and forced myself to deal with the real priority of the best strategy for a faster transition. I had been making slow decisions and sometimes no decisions during the time I allowed myself to resist what was needed, which to some degree, compromised trust and confidence from my management teams.

Once I intellectualized the best strategy forward, the harder work was to consciously manage my emotions so I wouldn't water down what I needed to do. I had identified the contracts we needed to discontinue before their dates of expiration to make room for us to focus time, energy, and resources on securing a new base of clients and standing up services for longer-term revenue and better profit. The projects I chose to release were the ones that had the lowest profit, had the highest demand, and consumed the most resources. The potential profit we could gain by fully moving into information technology was far greater than what was available through conference work. I needed to voluntarily let go of most of our conference contracts and move us in the right direction before more involuntary and undesirable experiences could blindside me.

The leap of faith Brad and I had taken two decades earlier wasn't that great of a leap—we had little to lose. The leap of faith I now faced was quite different. My lifestyle had blossomed into a life of comfort and an accumulation of "stuff," and I wanted to keep it that way. I liked the feeling of having and getting things that I wanted, when I wanted. The company provided my family with a pretty cushioned existence. Brad's salary in the local government job he accepted was far from what we needed to sustain the way we had become accustomed to living. So the choice I had to make to put the home life we'd built at risk was paralyzing. I was being challenged to put it all on the line. This was the internal war that looked like indecision to everyone else because I wasn't willing to admit my selfish paralysis to anyone other than Brad (who was completely disengaged). But eventually, I grew tired of the stress from my internal war and made a significant decision: to follow the soft voice inside telling me to trust myself more than I feared failure.

> **I made a significant decision: to follow the soft voice inside telling me to trust myself more than I feared failure.**

Metaphorically, there were two elevators. I was riding the elevator heading down (my old conference contracts), hoping to get off on the right floor, at the right time, to catch the elevator going up (new and more promising possibilities in the information technology market). If the speed of the elevator going down outpaced the timing of the elevator going up, we were going to have major problems.

I was in control of the two-elevator decision, but I was not completely in control of the timing.

I was also grappling with the composition and dynamics of the leadership team I had around me. Brad and I had each other as support for two decades; we didn't really need other generals. Together, we were pretty great at designing strategies, assembling teams, and deploying what was needed for success. But once Brad left, there was a big hole that needed to be filled. Brad and I were like the two sides of the brain, and I didn't realize the significance of this until he was gone. I wanted an experienced general who could replace his side, and think and do the part of the business I hadn't had to do. But that didn't happen. The leaders I had in this two-elevator scenario were not equipped to step in like I needed. This was not their fault. Like me, they had never seen or been through what we were facing, but more importantly, they hadn't signed up to own this challenge that otherwise would have been Brad and mine to own. I did a few early test discussions, and it didn't take long for me to figure out that their discomfort and anxiety would only make things more difficult. Being a committee of one was scary. At one point I got weak and went back to Brad to try and appeal to him again to come back.

"Brad," I said, trying to be as light and present in the moment as I could. "I need to talk to you about where we are in the business."

"Yeah." His one-word answer was a clear "please don't ask me" response. I didn't want to continue, but I stifled my pride.

"Running the company and trying to do the heavy lift of transitioning it without a CFO isn't going to work anymore," I said, thinking of the latest failed CFO hire. "There are critical decisions that need to be made as we balance the shift away from our conference contracts. I need your help."

I hated having to go back to Brad and ask for his help but felt pretty good that this time I managed to do it without accusation or frustration.

He met my energy and responded calmly and nicely as well. "You seem to be doing fine; you understand the numbers."

"Understanding the numbers isn't the problem. I need solid leadership for financial strategy and planning. We are not running the same business as before, and I'm no CPA. We've never found the right fit for this role since you left."

"Malitta, I know where this is headed, and you know I can't leave my job."

I had promised myself to stay calm but his response made me lose my battle with self-control. Before I knew it, I exploded, "Dammit! Who are you? You said you would come back, and all I ever get is your back when I ask. You're acting like your boss's little b****!"

Well, I probably don't need to describe how things went from there. It turned into one of the ugliest arguments we'd had in our entire marriage.

After that exchange, I wanted to walk out of the business and kick Brad out of our house. But for a reason I couldn't explain at the time, I couldn't bring myself to do either.

I was knee-deep in life-changing, first-time encounters, and it felt like everyone (both in the company and at home) expected me to have answers that would hold everything together. It made me empathetic toward first-term US presidents (okay, my situation was not quite that major, but I think you get the point). I was expected to know what to do about things I'd never encountered and be equipped to handle situations I had never been in, while everyone around watched and demanded success. Never had my company faced such a major operations and revenue crisis and never had my family had so much to lose. I felt the weight of keeping everyone safe and this drove me deeper into isolation.

It became more evident to me that the timing of my down and up elevators was off, so I had to face making more aggressive and undesirable adjustments. I first tried streamlining general company expenses, which helped, but the pressure was heating up. The margin between our income and spending was too narrow for comfort based on what was needed to build out our new services. So it was no longer a question about what to do but rather the best way to do it—I had to do a big chop. My main concern was about the impact the chop would have on morale and retention of staff we needed to keep for what was ahead. I knew that if I did not execute successfully, I could end up with more problems than I already had.

What I needed was a giant pause button. I wanted to neatly plan pivot strategies that aligned with the endless best practices filling my bookshelves, crowding my email inbox, and lodged in my brain from countless executive courses—but there wasn't enough time. There would be no neatly drafted plans based on predictive analytics or well-organized and time-phased actions. The luxury of time had lapsed, which meant that both the "what" and "how" options had narrowed.

To add to my headache, when I was busy resisting reality, I unconsciously operated in an unhealthy "under fire" mindset. I allowed (and even encouraged) my teams to chase rather than pursue work, even work that might have kept us more dependent on the elevator going down. Chasing meant that our focus was more on winning than on the alignment of what we were pursuing. We chased low-hanging fruit because it was easiest to grab and it camouflaged fear. My posture of panic and resistance as the CEO led the company into an ill-advised shotgun approach. As this was happening, I was convinced I had "no choice." These are two words that are now my warning signs. Any time I start to tell myself I have no choice, I know it is exactly a time when I need to *make* a choice.

I spent money and wasted time chasing distractions. I thought I couldn't get us from where we were to where we needed to be quickly enough, so I settled for bridges instead of pathways. I sought out solutions that could help carry me over my obstacle rather than through it. I told myself, and my people, that this way of operating would be temporary—just long enough to turn the tide and reestablish our footing. My leadership team had enough information to know the company was facing a revenue cliff and like me, they were anxious about their own security. So they eagerly jumped on board with the bridge-building solution. I knew we'd reached a bad place when we found ourselves managing conferences, community health outreach, transportation safety campaigns, information technology design, research support, and web and graphic projects all at the same time with an inadequate infrastructure and thinly spread resources.

But the bridges kept us busy. Having new work and new clients gave us the illusion of progress. Being busy was not productive. In many ways it was a form of regression. It muddied the waters and kept the most important obstacles out of immediate view. We were all over the place, and as the CEO, I had allowed this to happen because I didn't want to step up and fully bet on that up elevator. I procrastinated because I didn't like its half-empty "potential." I sat in my office one night reviewing a set of reports from our contracts manager. The reports spoke volumes about the lack of synergy and clarity my leadership was producing. We had too many different skills spread across unrelated streams of revenue—scaling for growth was an impossibility. The only thing that was clear from those reports was that we were chasing dollars, and I needed to put an end to it. I knew that night that if I didn't stop to make sure only the right things made it onto our up elevator, I would sabotage any possibility for success. The internal switch I needed kicked in, and I started to shift from a mindset driven by fear that had me grasping to hold on, to feeling like I couldn't let go fast enough.

I slept very little that night, but this time it was because I was anxious, not worried. Once I made the mental shift to let go, the worry seemed to dissipate. I called an early morning meeting with my executive team and told them that our season of doing the comb-over was ending. I said, "We are balding, and our bald areas are expanding and becoming impossible to ignore." I told them to evaluate their departments and return within one week with a list of recommendations for service and position eliminations. My goal was to expedite cuts that would position us for smart growth and improve our bottom line. I told them there would be no sacred cows, everyone and every contract needed to be evaluated objectively for alignment with the company's long-term direction for services and profit.

Detaching my personal feelings and heeding my own directive about having no sacred cows was hard. I had to focus on where we needed to land and not the process I was going to have to go through to get there. I also had to remain conscious of my thoughts and emotions (in that order). My thoughts drove my emotions. If I thought fear, I felt afraid. If I thought hurt, I felt pain. And, if I thought of failure, I felt doubtful. Those were error thoughts, and error thinking produces emotions that can block objectivity. Objectivity was the very thing I needed to combat unproductive mind chatter that wanted to keep ego sensitivities, relationships, appearances, and the temptation to stay in what was comfortable in the moment as priorities.

I finally felt more consciously connected to what was really needed. My biggest task was to stay true to being the CEO of the company and not CEO to individual agendas (including my own). There were many loyal employees I wanted to protect and who wanted me to protect them. I can't count the number of drive-by "Hello, I just wanted to check in" visits I got once the buzz and energy of streamlining spread. People were afraid, and so was I. They wanted assurances I couldn't give them, and I also could not give them the full picture. I wasn't ready. Many of the ones coming to see me were people I knew well. I knew their children and had celebrated and mourned life with them. We'd been together for a long time. But I had to accept what life was showing me—that people and ways of life must sometimes be released. When they are not, new paths for what is best can be missed.

Some of the people I needed to part ways with I hadn't known as long, and they were on my executive team. The need to release them had more to do with fit than finances. This was my fault. I'd hired a few in a state of desperation and chaos. They had technical skills, and in that regard, they were good but, overall, they were not good for us. As in other areas, I was forced to face and not excuse or justify this any longer for convenience. This was true for one executive in particular.

When I hired this executive, I knew he was not a good fit, but I felt I had few to no choices because I desperately needed to offload several of the balls I was juggling. I was uneasy about his energy during our first encounter, but I talked myself away from that sensation and, instead, justified a decision to hire him by telling myself he could help move us away from a posture of entitlement that was creeping into our culture. I told myself I needed someone like him to help kick people into action and enforce more accountability. (Remember, my mindset was in fight mode.) This was the basis for the decision to hire him.

The mistake of this decision became painfully obvious after I began to challenge everyone on my executive team to make recommendations for service and staff cuts. It was clear that this executive was skilled in delivering uncomfortable demands when those demands left him and his people unscathed. He was not cut out for the difficult path of sharing in the pain that was ahead, and his attitude and energy began to show it. He expressed his anger and anxiety by making snarky, passive-aggressive comments. The part of him I had talked myself into had boomeranged.

To prepare for the cuts, my executive team and I were gathering often to discuss strategy and narrow the list of positions to be eliminated and people to be laid off. During one of our final meetings, I expressed how difficult a decision it was for me to downsize the business. I shared stories of how Brad and I had built the company, our vision for its existence, and my feelings about releasing people who had been with us since the beginning. I made myself vulnerable, and for the first time in the presence of anyone other than myself, I teared up and I could hear my voice quiver. I didn't feel embarrassed about it; I wanted a moment of truth with them. It was important to me for them to understand how personal these decisions were to me. I needed them to treat what we were doing with great care.

The response and comments I received after being vulnerable in that meeting were compassionate, with the exception of that one executive. His countenance was unpleasant, and his vibration felt condescending. I had a brief sensation of embarrassment for having been so open but quickly reminded myself how insignificant his judgment of me was. I had already spent too much time thinking of me.

Two days after that meeting, as I headed toward the conference room for the final meeting about the layoff plan, I bumped into him.

"Good morning," I said.

"Good morning," he replied, uncharacteristically chipper.

I was clearly anxious and not thrilled about the circumstances. I said to him, "There are plenty of other things I'd rather be discussing today."

He snickered. "Well time for you to put your big girl pants on."

I'm not violent, but I felt I could have been in that moment. I'd tolerated him much too long.

Brené Brown says people misunderstand vulnerability. Vulnerability, as she describes, is not weakness. To the contrary, she describes it as an accurate measurement of courage.[1] Apparently, this executive misinterpreted my vulnerability. Maybe I went too far when I shared my feelings in that meeting two days prior, but I had *chosen* the path of authenticity and that felt right for me. We were about to do the second layoff in the history of the company, and this time it was my decision. Without warning, 35 percent of our workforce was about to be unemployed. Even worse, after looking closely at our financials, I made the decision that paying severance to 35 percent of our workforce was not in the company's best interest. No warning, no severance. I was disgusted by the situation but determined.

I wasn't quite sure if that executive meant for me to actually hear his "big pants" comment as I continued to walk toward the conference room, but I did, and as soon as that meeting was over, I added his name to my list.

Vulnerability isn't necessarily what some people want to see in a leader, including others who sat around my conference table. That one executive just happened to let it show. I looked weak when he wanted to see toughness. But I was tired of having to be a tough leader just so our tough situation could make people like him feel okay. The people losing their jobs didn't need us as the leadership team to be tough. They needed us to demonstrate compassion, empathy, honor, and care, and I had to lead by example.

I sat alone in the office that night and signed off on the list of layoffs after adding the names of a few executives. Only Brad could have understood the magnitude of the moment, but he was far from where I sat.

Learning to Observe

A mentor once told me that a situation or circumstance has a way of becoming what you choose to call it, so be careful how you label things. She said, "If you call something an obstacle, then it will be exactly that. There is a significant difference between an obstacle and a challenge." A simple but important perspective I decided to live by. Every time I mindlessly label something an obstacle, I experience inner chaos and added stress in trying to deal with it. The very thought of having an obstacle triggers a negative energy within me, signaling a reaction rooted in the fear of some type of threat. And when I operate from a mindset of threat, I give my problem-driven thoughts and emotions far too much control. Observance allows me to avoid this pitfall.

My decision to do the layoff is a clear example. I suffered for weeks, operating mostly from within my feelings. I dreaded facing the hurt and disappointment from the people who would be affected and imagined the experience of it several times before it even happened. Of course, I'm not suggesting that I should not have had feelings or thoughts about the circumstance; I believe empathy is the emotion that keeps humanity bonded. But had I been more conscious about operating as an objective observer of the circumstance rather than a participant in the circumstance, I would have focused on the anticipated agony less. I would have suffered through the weeks leading up to it less. As a participant, I saw an obstacle. As an observer, I saw a solution. One posture focuses on what is wrong, the other on what is possible. My father used to tell me this when I was young: "Whatever it is you will wish you had done ten years from now *is* what you should do now."

D-Day: The Bigger Layoff

The $17 million contract layoff was something we had six months to plan and execute. This was a quite different situation. I woke up the morning of the bigger layoff with my stomach in knots.

As managers notified staff and executives notified managers, I also notified executives. The layoff process resulted in pandemonium and took me through three of the slowest and most excruciating hours of my career. Some cried, some were very angry, and others were in shock. At the end of that long day, I sat in my office and gave myself permission to cry. My tears were a rush of emotions not just about the layoffs but the way my entire life seemed to be unraveling.

After I pulled myself together from the release of emotions and tears, I continued to sit at my desk almost motionless well into the dark of evening. Everyone had long left for the day, and the office was unnervingly quiet. I walked around reliving the chaos from the day, trying to wrap my mind around everything that had happened. The emotional rip of the Band-Aid was evident as I looked at the many cubicles and offices that had been hastily cleared. It was almost too much to take in, especially alone, but sometimes pain is strangely soothing. I wanted to hold on to it for a while and feel everything again—it seemed too significant of an event to just allow it to be over. Was I just supposed to move on after part of my life's work had crumbled—after I let down so many people who had entrusted the company and me with their livelihood? I stayed in the office for several more hours, unable to detach myself from the day's emotions, knowing the cutting I needed to do was not yet over. I was going to have to face what needed to happen next to keep moving the company toward its future. As Spencer Johnson puts it, "The quicker you let go of old cheese, the sooner you find new cheese."[2]

I'd cleared a pathway. We had fewer staff, a smaller payroll, and an overall reduction in expenses. My two elevators were in better motion but we still had a couple of large expenses slowing the pace of progress, one of which was our office lease. Between the layoff related to the $17 million contract loss and my decision to lay off another 35 percent of our workforce, we were left operating in office space that was far more than what we needed. I knew that in addition to paying for more space than we needed, having empty offices and cubicles would make our work environment feel like a graveyard. It would be a daily reminder of the death we'd gone through. Too much space, too many bad reminders, and too much rent, but I still had a year and a half left on our 15,000-square-foot lease.

Too much space and bad memories were one thing, but also the math didn't work, and I knew it all too well. I had run and rerun the numbers, and our rent was the hole in the donut—the last big expense I needed to adjust to get better cadence between my up and down elevators. I called the landlord to negotiate, and he shut me down before I could fully get out my rehearsed request. So I still had a significant problem. I asked myself: What do I choose to do? The answer I came up with was "Go home and open a bottle of wine." So I did. I had no other answers, so I accepted the lease and rent as part of the picture for the company's future.

PROVE IT LESSON

When faced with a challenge, practice being an observer (not a participant) to create the best solution. Examine what you are experiencing as though you are watching and advising someone else. Obstacles block and hinder; challenges are an invitation to take new action.

PROVE IT QUESTIONS

- Do I operate with an open mind (focus on possibilities and not problems) when challenges rise?

- Do I allow my feelings about a situation to overpower my thoughts and drive my actions?

- Do I observe objectively (as though it were not me in a situation) and allow myself to create with an open mind, without attachment to an expected outcome?

PROVE IT MINDFUL PRACTICES

Write down the biggest challenges you currently face and the barriers (in your mind) blocking your ability to move beyond them. After you have this list, imagine advising someone else with the exact same challenges and then write down what you would tell them to do.

For the comprehensive PROVE IT Mindshifts Journaling Guide, please refer to the appendix.

CHAPTER 4

VICTIM TO VALOR

Excavation: to dig out and remove; to expose to view by, or as if by, digging away a covering
—*MERRIAM-WEBSTER DICTIONARY*

SO FAR, I'VE SHARED A lot about my journey and mindshifting related to the business, but I haven't shared many details about the journey at home. In this chapter (and the next), I tell you more about the introspection and self-work I had to do to stay in my marriage.

Choosing to Be the Victim

I wanted to hate Brad. In fact, for a period of time, I did hate Brad. What he did, the way he left me in such an awful situation and never looked back, was unfathomable to me. The last thing I intended or wanted was to move past his betrayal. I described his departure before as devastating, but that doesn't come close to describing how low I felt and how much my respect had plummeted for the person I trusted most.

I was operating in a space of deep hurt and disappointment; life was very dark for me during that time. My home had gone from being a safe space of companionship, love, and support to one of volatility, anger, and emotional instability. I couldn't understand Brad—what would make him just walk away? We'd built the business together, and it was such an intricate part of our life together. It felt like he'd walked out on us—our marriage and our family. But he insisted that was not the case. I lived on a pendulum of emotions that swung from hurt to rage.

I'll give you a little background on how Brad's job opportunity unfolded. A close friend had won an election to run our county's government. The friend heavily pursued Brad to join his administration. He threw every flattery and legal bait he could to get Brad to accept his offer. He was a politician, and like many politicians, he was masterful at flattery and appealing to people's egos, and Brad was no exception.

As this was happening, I didn't give it much of my attention because Brad taking a job was, in my mind, about as possible as an elephant learning to fly. This is why I had such difficulty orienting my thoughts the day Brad walked into my office and announced he was leaving. It took minutes for his words to register and for me to process the significance of what was happening. Before that day in my office, I believed Brad and I both thought the offer had been laughable. But at some point, Brad stopped laughing, and I didn't notice. Brad chose to believe his friend's flattery and justified his decision to leave, saying he was "the only one" who could help his friend get the job done. In time, I would learn how his friend's words filled a thirst in Brad that I didn't know existed. But all I could think when Brad blindsided me with his news was that this job was a convenient exit strategy for him. It felt like Brad's way of escaping the daunting transition needed to avoid the revenue cliff the company faced.

Fixed in that mindset, all that mattered to me was the damage Brad was causing and the disregard he had for me as he was causing it. I saw everything through a lens of anger and betrayal combined with a new view of him as a self-centered and arrogant person I could no longer trust. This made our home life pretty disastrous. I watched Brad inhale the smoke of praise his new job blew his way (and there was a lot of it) as I took daily beatings to defend our family's income and foundation. In my eyes, Brad was playing local politics (for basically no money), and I was fighting for our lives. I was mad.

From my perspective, I had given Brad every ounce of support he ever needed or asked for when the business had been *his* passion and *his* source of identity. I willingly took the second seat and put in the muscle we'd needed to get our company up and running. I worked tirelessly writing two hundred-plus page proposals (that was before streamlined procurement was a thing), created and led operations, traveled back-to-back for weeks on end, and functioned as co-CEO (behind closed doors). And when I left to pursue my own passion, I willingly shut down my nonprofit and returned to the company within a day of realizing it was at risk because the COO we hired wasn't working out.

I'd even given in and gone along with the company having Brad's name despite the fact that it was *our* company—something we built together from the ground up. As mentioned earlier, I was willing to do what was necessary to move the company forward, and that included living with the external perception that the company was Brad's. Of course, this bothered me to a degree during different seasons of the business, but the full magnitude of resentment didn't come to light until he decided to leave me in something he enjoyed taking credit for when things were going well. But now (in my mind) that we faced an uphill battle, one that we could possibly lose, he wanted me to "take over." The new Brad I was seeing became a trigger that caused me to implode. I was sleeping next to a stranger I didn't like and wasn't sure I could love.

There was rarely a day that didn't begin with me beating Brad down with insults, hurling my pain at him trying to make him feel what I was feeling. We argued and I fussed to no avail. I wallowed in our big mess hoping Brad would miraculously come to his senses and own up to what he'd done. In anger, I thought badgering would somehow convince him to walk away from all the accolades and glory he was getting in his new life and come back to me in my pain and misery and help rescue us. I couldn't understand why he was okay with letting me carry the heavy load for our family because I didn't understand (nor did I care) what he needed.

Regardless of *Brad's* needs or reasons at the time (something I could not control), *my* situation was still the same. Stress and anger were in control, and my daily experience was a recurring blur of bad stuff. I adjusted to living with headaches, and the highlight of my days became the sprint home for a glass of wine. Over time, in my eyes, the people in my company didn't appear to be much different from Brad. They too started to feel like leeches who needed to take life from me to keep themselves alive (harsh I know, but this was my story at the time). I felt like I was expected to keep everyone else's livelihood safe and secure while my own was questionable. Did anyone get this? Did anyone care? It didn't seem so.

This was my victim narrative. The one that drove my thoughts and actions. Not only did I repeat this to myself; I believed it. It was the reality my mind created, and I lived in this paradigm for almost two years until an experience one morning shook me out of it.

I was on my elliptical, and in the middle of my workout, I started praying and arguing with God. I was so angry. I went into a loud rant about how unfair things were in my life. I yelled at God for not answering my many prayers and seemingly having no care or concern for what I was going through. I asked God (literally), "Why have you given me such a bitter cup in life? What am I being punished for?" Yes, I actually said "bitter cup," and I wasn't finished. "I give, I support, I'm honest. What in the world more do you want from me?" And before I could get another victim declaration out of my mouth, I heard an immediate response that I won't label as divine (to save us all from debate), but the words were clear and didn't come from that loud angry voice in my own head. It was a soft, loving voice that said, "Why are you choosing to drink from it? Just put it down."

Esther Hicks once said, "What you think and what you get is always a perfect vibrational match, so it can be very helpful to make a conscious correlation between what you are thinking and what is manifesting."[1]

Leaning into Valor

What happened that morning on my elliptical stunned me. It snatched away the cozy blanket I'd wrapped myself in that kept me covered as a victim. The message was eerily clear and left no room for misinterpretation. I had chosen self-pity and in many unconscious ways had been seeking sympathy for my problems. Self-pity gave me permission to hold on to anger, and it justified my resentment—two things I didn't want to let go of. They had become my companions, a soothing fix for my hurt feelings. But now I could see they were a trap. I was choosing to suffer. Victimhood blocked me from accepting responsibility for my own choices—the ones I'd already made that culminated in what I was experiencing and the ones I would make moving forward.

Brad had made his decision. Any additional focus on that was going to be a waste of time and a drain of my energy. Enough wasting and draining had already happened. I had been attached to a view of Brad as the perpetrator, so I had put in a lot of effort to keep that view alive. I had made sure the injustice he inflicted was remembered every day, but the only person stirred by my efforts had been me. The author of *The Untethered Soul*, Michael Singer, describes this kind of experience as one where we keep something alive because it bothers us so much.[2]

It was as if I couldn't move on until I could get someone, anyone, to understand. What a waste of energy. No one was ever going to understand the way I wanted them to because no one can ever fully experience the feelings of another. The best we can hope for is that another person can *imagine* being in our situations, having had all our prior experiences in life, with an awareness of our unique makeup of emotions, and then *guess* how we must feel. This is so hard to find that some of us settle for the consoling option of pity—for ourselves and from others. Pity gives us permission to go into our pain and lay in it without guilt or feeling responsible for doing something to change our perspective. Some of us have been seeking pity since childhood to justify carrying anger and resentment we don't want to let go of.

I didn't realize what I had been doing in my own situation until the soft words rang clear. "Just put it down." If I wanted to get out of my suffering, I was going to have to choose to not suffer. No matter what happens outside me, I always hold the power of choosing how it affects what's inside me.

Valor is having courage in the face of threat or danger—it's about personal bravery, particularly when in battle. I was definitely in a battle, but I was convinced that the battle was about saving the business and getting Brad to acknowledge and accept responsibility for his betrayal. The real battle, which was actually much more difficult, was the one within myself. Winning this battle required me to accept, forgive, and move on.

I had always hated the phrase "forgiveness is not for the other person, it's for you," but nothing could have been truer. I had myself locked in a cycle of suffering that I was never going to get out of as long as I believed I was there because of someone else (Brad). I didn't choose all the changes happening around me, but I was unconsciously choosing to hold on to negative thoughts and feelings about them. I was *choosing* to be a victim. Nelson Mandela said it best: "I realized that when I went through that gate, if I still hated . . . they would still have me. I wanted to be free. And so, I let it go."[3]

I had options for freeing myself from victimhood, and in a deeply emotional state, I considered the extremes. I thought about leaving Brad after convincing myself that his actions were more about me than him—that is, a reflection of how much he did or did not love me. I also considered walking away from the business leaving loose ends untied—letting others (including Brad) feel the impact I'd been feeling in trying to hold everything together. These were my two options for escaping.

But as I mentioned before, I could never bring myself to do either. Escaping never felt like the right answer for me. At first, I thought it was because I was too chicken to walk away and let it all go, but eventually I came to understand that walking away would have been easier to do. Walking away would have been the chicken's way out. Staying was much harder and scared me more. So why did I stay? I knew I would feel worse about myself had I run. There was no valor in running. I'd already let myself down enough, and I didn't want to do that again. There is a quote that is attributed to Albert Einstein that says, "You cannot solve a problem with the same mind that created it." I had to look at myself and shift into a new mindset.

I hadn't been open to any of this before my elliptical mindshift moment. Being a victim made it easier to deal with all my fears, unhappiness, and internal torment. As the victim, rejection and failure are understandable and maybe even acceptable because nothing can be a *victim's* fault. Again, none of this thinking was conscious. Blame was so natural that I didn't see it for what it was at all. Sure, a lot had happened at the hands of others, but that was no match for what I was allowing to happen by my own hands. External events and circumstances had hijacked my thinking, and I was the part of the problem that would have followed me out of either door of escape—the company or my marriage to Brad.

It was major progress for me to realize the self-work I needed to own. And the realization was timely. It happened several months after we completed the second layoff when things had calmed a bit. But right in the middle of my big *aha* moment and embrace of the need to shift from victimhood, life kept happening, and I got another curveball. My company was awarded a highly coveted information technology contract that gave us an opportunity to increase our revenue to nine figures—this was part of our plan for the elevator that was going up. The competition to get this contract had been tough. This was a much-needed win for the trajectory of revenue but also for our confidence about the future. Personally, this win restored a level of self-confidence *I* needed after some of the beatings I'd taken. Even Brad showed up the day we celebrated this win—it was big.

But two days before I was scheduled to travel out of town with my team to attend a big kickoff conference for the contract, I received a call and was told that our contract award was being contested and we would be disqualified unless we could disprove the complaint. A competitor company that had lost challenged our award, alleging we were ineligible based on a technicality. We had worked for more than a year to win this contract, and again, our future depended on it. It was the biggest gamble of the elevator plan I bet on when the decision was made to release much of our remaining base of conference work.

I hung up the phone and sat in my office in disbelief. I didn't know what to do. I was trying to operate in a more positive space, but I'm not sure I'd ever felt so unloved and unprotected in my life. With all the other unsettling moves that had happened in the company, I couldn't imagine sharing this latest blow—not even with my executive team. The office-wide announcement and celebration of our win made the situation even more difficult. I decided to hold the information. I needed time to fight back my own bad thoughts before inviting everyone else's worry and stress into my headspace. I was told during the call that I had thirty days to pull together our response to defend ourselves against the ruling, but until then, we were unable to perform on the contract. I said nothing to my team and moved forward with our trip to the kickoff conference.

When I arrived at the conference, the place was buzzing with energy. The contract awarded included about fifty companies and people were almost giddy—it was an opportunity to make a lot of money. There were several hundred people at the conference, and it felt like everybody but me was excited to be there. My team was as eager as the rest; their energy was high and upbeat, so I had no choice but to fake my mood and do my best to camouflage feeling like an impostor. This should have been a big day for me, and it took a lot of self-talk not to pity party my way back to my hotel room and hide.

As I checked in at the registration table, a program administrator who had been on the contract review committee recognized the name of our company on my badge. She touched my arm and said, "Excuse me, but didn't anyone contact you to let you know your company has been disqualified from participating on the contract? You shouldn't be here." Anxiety, embarrassment, and then panic. I quickly tried to step out of earshot of my team, but she continued to speak, loudly, as if I hadn't understood her the first time: "You're not allowed to attend this conference."

I felt like time had stopped.

Everything started to run through my mind, from the moment Brad walked out until now. I needed something or someone to blame. I needed to soothe and get rid of what I was feeling. The last thing I wanted in those moments was to be positive and courageous. I wanted Brad to show up and take responsibility for all of my embarrassment, fear, and disappointment.

These thoughts flooded my mind while she stood there waiting for me to say something. Then, as though she could feel my thoughts, her face relaxed and her energy seemed to soften. I asked her if we could step aside and speak privately. We walked a few feet away, and I explained that I had gotten a late call two days prior and was told we had thirty days to appeal and prove our eligibility. She still stood her ground and said, until that time, we were not eligible to do business with them, and therefore, we were not allowed to attend the conference.

I scrambled for words, unable to process having to tell my team we would have to pack and go home. I told her that no one said during the call that we could not attend the conference, and because none of what our competitor asserted had been proven (and was very much an error), my team and I deserved and needed to attend the conference. After a couple of minutes of discussion, she paused and agreed to let us participate. The two-day conference was a great event for my team. My body was there but my mind and emotions were elsewhere.

By the time I got back from the conference, I was clearer about what needed to be done. I was tired of dealing with challenges, but I could feel myself growing, which made their pain more bearable. I was becoming a better person, someone I was proud of and liked again. I was responding more consciously and reacting less emotionally. When I was approached at the conference, the negative thoughts crept up, but they did not win and control my response. That was progress. I was discovering the power of getting the encouragement and support I once sought from sources outside me from within me. I was shifting away from *expecting* external help. If it happened, great, but I stopped looking for it. And oddly enough, just as I leaned into this new mindset, the universe sent unexpected help proving the theory that if you really want something, try attracting it, not chasing it.

Proving our eligibility to be part of that contract required digging through ten years of financial records. To my surprise, when I told Brad what I needed to do, he stepped in. Brad worked in the office with me in the evenings and on the weekends for several weeks, and together we pulled the data and records needed for our appeal. We were successful, and the contract was finalized. This was the first time since he'd left that Brad got involved in anything related to the company. His presence was temporary, but he gave me what was needed at the time. My victim mindset wasn't completely gone and tempted me on some of those days with negative thoughts. But it didn't win. I felt more gratitude than anything, and to my surprise, I had the courage to thank Brad instead of soothing any lingering resentment by punishing him with guilt.

Forgiving was the most courageous thing I had to do. But it wasn't about forgiving Brad; it was about forgiving myself. As I said before, Brad hadn't been my real problem. In my efforts to be the person I thought I needed to be to have what I thought I wanted, I fell into a pattern of unconsciously giving away my power and agreeing to suppress important parts of who I am. I was intellectually committed to following the path to success, but I was not inspirationally grounded. Meaning, my mind calculated what I needed to do to achieve what the world commonly labels as success, but I did not monitor the balance between that calculation, my happiness, and my experience of fulfillment. This is how regret comes to life. I gave my mind full control and trained my spirit to cooperate and follow its lead. My approach should have been the opposite.

Forgiving was the most courageous thing I had to do. But it wasn't about forgiving Brad; it was about forgiving myself.

Forgiving myself and getting past the regret took courage. I had to take responsibility, but I couldn't beat myself (or anyone else) up and stay angry about it. I had to keep the lesson but release the mistake. This meant shifting away from a practice of reliving events. Things happen—sometimes bad things—but that's life. My experience of anything is most greatly affected by my answer to this question: What do I choose to do about it *now*? The present moment is the most important moment. Yesterday is finished, and tomorrow is a mystery. The gift is in the present moment—to choose consciously in ways that can produce what is *ultimately* most desired. My now moments are building blocks; nothing is more important. This is what I didn't honor before as I gave small pieces of myself away, and this is what caused my mind and spirit to be out of alignment—the soul of who I am—divided.

Forgiveness in my marriage had to happen as well. To stay in it, I had to let go of the ugliness and put it in my past. This was a real decision. There were plenty of days I felt putting it all in the past was not just unfair but also undoable. But pushing myself to think more clearly, I eventually embraced that, married or not, Brad would always be in my life. We were too connected on too many levels. Dragging bad memories and resentment into our future was not going to be good for us or our family. Besides, I still loved him deeply. As I slowly let my guard down and gave myself permission to have these softer feelings and thoughts, I became conscious of not allowing the happiness and success he found without me to trigger my pain.

I began to work really hard to "put the cup down" (the words I heard after fussing at God on the elliptical that morning). I knew it was important for me to forgive, and I needed help to get there. I read a lot, and one story I read stuck with me: the story of Joyce Meyer.[4] Her father had sexually, mentally, and verbally abused her until she left home at the age of eighteen. She not only forgave him but also later took care of him and her mother (who she says never came to her rescue during the years of abuse). I couldn't imagine that level of forgiveness and was immediately moved and inspired about my own situation. I was struggling to forgive something that in the scheme of things was pretty insignificant. Joyce Meyer modeled for me what was possible.

The hell I'd been in was coming from the inside, but the key to getting out was there as well. Getting rid of my hurt feelings was no one's responsibility but mine. I have control of choosing what to hold inside. The story of Joyce Meyer helped me see there is emotional freedom in not holding on to pain and resentment, but it also enlightened me to the fact that shame can be in the shadows playing a part as well. I realized I was taking it personally that the company was no longer doing as well as it had, and I was blaming *myself* for it. There was an element of shame compounding what I was experiencing.

According to Joyce Meyer, after years of feeling embarrassment and shame, she came to understand that what her dad had done was about him and not her. Her challenge, as the victim of his actions, was to reconcile *her* experience of him dealing with his own issues. Brad's decision to leave the company was a decision that was about him. I was not his focal point; nor was the company. My task was to reconcile *my* experience of Brad living out his truth. He hadn't set out to hurt me. I wasn't an intentional victim of his actions; I was collateral damage. Clearly, Brad wasn't thinking about me—he was thinking about himself. And whether I like this truth or not, he and everyone else living has that freedom. Maybe it was selfish of him, but calling it selfish wasn't going to stop my pain. Not taking it personally was what was going to put an end to it.

In addition to understanding the value of not taking it personally, I learned another lesson that was not overnight for me. That is why the title of this chapter is "Victim to Valor." I was invested in my victim posture. I felt letting go of the emotions I'd gone through would be letting Brad off the hook for what he'd done. I was afraid that if I forgave him, I'd somehow be giving a stamp of approval and permission for him to forget everything that had happened between us. It felt like a form of self-betrayal to let the impact of something so devastating to me to be forgotten. But to make sure it was not forgotten, I had to keep remembering, which required me to keep reliving it all. That is self-inflicted suffering and the opposite of peace. I had to have the courage to choose peace.

There were tough questions I had to answer to do this: What if I change my own narrative? What if I let go of my old story of betrayal and replace it with a new one, such as "Brad found an opportunity that makes him happy, and I am happy for him"? What if I begin to accept what he tells me as truth, that he has confidence in me and believes I can do what is needed for the company? What if I believe him when he tells me that none of what he's done is to hurt me? What if I have the courage to do this, to let go of my hurt emotions and replace them with empathy for Brad? What if I could quiet the voice in my head screaming that my forgiveness of this situation would be a weakness? What if I could stop thinking and behaving like a victim?

Unconsciously, I focused on being a survivor within my crisis instead of getting out of it. I had mastered being a victim. When I reached a point of frustration when Brad and I were running the company together, I told myself that because of him, I was trapped in a role I didn't want and I was underappreciated. When Brad left the company, I found myself repeating the same narrative. Brad had moved on; the only person trapping and underappreciating me was myself. I was trying to shift things back to the way they had been when the way they had been wasn't even what I wanted. I let the hurt I felt about Brad's departure dictate my experience of it.

I was never a victim; it was just more soothing and comfortable to behave like one.

PROVE IT LESSON

Being a victim is not just about the thing that happened to you (that is major) but also about the state of mind you're left in after it has happened. Carrying negative emotions and bad memories can create a victimhood trap; it takes valor to choose to release them. When we choose to remind and hold up the offenses of our offenders, we choose to remind and hold up the offenses within ourselves. Of course, some trauma must be supported with professional help. If you are unable to move into a space of peace about your experiences, consider possible options for getting the support you need to get to a better place.

PROVE IT QUESTIONS

- What makes me hold on to and relive bad experiences?
- What am I in need of and what would it take to release these experiences?
- In what ways is the resentment, anger, or pain negatively showing up and affecting my life?

PROVE IT MINDFUL PRACTICES

Write down what you find yourself remembering that brings you pain. Note the places, people, or experiences that trigger those thoughts. Consider if there is something you can do in the present to dismantle the memory so you can leave it behind you. For example, instead of reliving the emotions I felt in the aftermath of Brad's decision, I choose to honor the thought that he was being the best person he was able to be given who he was at the time—and I stop there, resisting any thoughts beyond that. This practice allows me to avoid replaying the anger and pain. Seek out positive support.

For the comprehensive PROVE IT Mindshifts Journaling Guide, please refer to the appendix.

CHAPTER 5

EGO IMBALANCE TO EGO CONSCIOUSNESS

> Your personality, which is conditioned by the past, then becomes your prison. . . . Your story becomes who you perceive yourself to be.
> —ECKHART TOLLE, *A NEW EARTH*

THE EGO IS DIFFICULT TO tame. Its mission is to protect the survival of the self, and in doing so, it must compare—constantly evaluating the degree of safety around us for survival. This can stir unconscious behaviors of superiority or inferiority.

After accepting that I needed to *completely* forgive so I could shift out of a victim mindset, I had to deal with the stuff I had nurtured that had gotten me there. This *stuff* wasn't pretty. I would have preferred working around it and not through it, but that isn't the way inner work happens.

I had to be honest with myself and focus my attention on the one person having the biggest impact on how I was experiencing life: me.

Excavating "Me"

I started to see the significant role my ego was playing. This came as a surprise to me. Like most people I know, ego was something I associated with people who needed attention, compliments, and a sense of elevation over others. Admittedly, I was prideful and fairly sensitive about being respected, but seeking attention and needing to feel superior was not something I struggled with. So the concept of having to deal with an ego issue never occurred to me. It was only after reading many books and studying the role of the ego more closely that I began to grasp its impact.

Sigmund Freud defined the ego as the decision-making part of the personality that mediates between our id, which is our primitive impulse thinking and instincts for survival and pleasure, and our superego, which is where more conscious thoughts are generated to align with values in society so we can create experiences of reward (or punishment). As I contemplated this definition, it became painfully clear how much my ego was out of balance. Although I had been ruled by my superego during the years I worked to achieve success (aligning my actions with social standards and an expectation of certain rewards for my efforts), the crisis I faced after Brad's departure and the threat of the revenue cliff kicked my id (survival instincts) into action with great intensity. My ego, the mediator between my id and superego, was not balanced, and this had a significant impact on my focus and actions.

First, let me explain my superego issue. I had fallen into a pattern of relying on external factors to form my opinions about myself (not too uncommon). When I was doing this, I was aware that other people's opinions about me mattered, but I wasn't conscious of how those opinions were manifesting. I'd developed a codependency that resulted in *unconscious* molding in response to the external applause or rejection I received. I did this in exchange for physical security (money and success) and emotional gratification (recognition and praise which reinforced that I was on the *right* track). Most of us do this; it is a system of cohabitation that a lot of humanity lives by. The challenge isn't that we do this but the degree to which we do. For me, it started with an innocent goal—to create a *good life*. But the more of the good life I created, the more I wanted. This required more and more molding to fit outside demands.

At some point, my happiness became dependent on how well I was controlling my outside world and what it was giving back to me in return. This made me what my mentor calls "disturbable." When things wouldn't go as I thought I needed them to, even something as minor as getting a flat tire, my entire energy and outlook for the day could turn bad. The flat tire might have taken an extra hour out of my day, but rather than feeling grateful for having resources to get it fixed, and getting it fixed quickly, my mind would stay stuck on the fact that it happened at all. Why? Because moments like getting a flat tire weren't part of the deal—they weren't factored into my expectations. When these types of moments happened, they disturbed my happiness. My happiness depended on things looking and unfolding as I expected them to. This is why I played my cards with the world so carefully. The agreement was that it would give me what it was supposed to in a way I expected if I gave myself to it the way it required. (Not very different from the agreement I thought I had with Brad.)

So I molded. That was part of the bargain I had with my outside world. When I faced this realization and examined how much of my *self* I'd compromised, I felt more alone than I had since the start of my crisis. I was still in the throes of transitioning the business, so doing this self-work at the same time made everything I was going through that much more difficult. In some ways, I wished I hadn't opened that box—that I'd left myself in a space of pretending the inner conflict I felt was normal. But the turn in the business and the shift in dynamics with Brad seemed to go hand in hand with a journey of self-realization, and the truth about how much the safety and happiness game was costing me, rather than giving me, further ignited my inner discontent. No surprise, I felt drained.

Happy moments can be generated from the outside, but happiness can only come from the inside. Happiness is a state of being; it isn't something that is sustained by careers, relationships, and the accumulation of money in our bank accounts. Yes, those things can create happy seasons or moments in our lives, but those things can also change instantly and in ways beyond our control. They are not safe places to plant seeds for happiness. Being happy despite what is happening in life is a decision. Yet we pray for it as if it is something that needs to show up. It is a gift we are born with that many of us overlook. If I commit to staying in a state of happiness (disconnecting my energy from life's highs and lows—and life will happen!), I have a better chance of living a life of contentment. Events like losing clients, disagreements in relationships, getting a flat tire, or even stubbing my toe are things I know will happen every now and then. So why is it that when they actually do, they have the power to sap feelings of happiness? True happiness isn't so easily derailed.

Happy moments can be generated from the outside, but happiness can only come from the inside.

Before I came to understand the difference between something making me happy and *being* happy, I orchestrated my life to control what I thought could create it. But happiness is an energy, and energy cannot be created; it can only be transformed and transferred. When I didn't get this, I tried muscling the company to operate at its peak and goading Brad to come back to his senses and get us back to a state of harmony. I thought if I could get everything in place in the right way with the right timing, I would be happy. But as I evolved on my journey, it was clear that neither of those events could make me happy—they would only temporarily satisfy my need to protect my security. And even as I grew in consciousness about this error way of thinking, I struggled. I was programmed to operate with the mindset that to have certain things, I *had* to do certain things, even if doing those things meant absorbing, creating, and living in bad spaces of energy every day.

Who in their right and conscious mind would *choose* to live this way?

I would watch my idea of happiness walk around outside me, and I would chase it, time and again, sometimes thinking I'd caught it, only for it to last for a season or moment. Inevitably, at least one of my requirements would shift out of place. My career, marriage, family dynamics, friendships, achievements, and finances never seemed to cooperate and stay in place all at the same time, so my happiness ebbed and flowed. Some call this life; they practice happiness as a variable that is contingent on possessions, money, events, relationships, and other external circumstances. I prefer the more consistent and less variable path of keeping a positive outlook, staying untethered and remaining open to the possibilities of how life might unfold, and responding with choices rather than reacting with feelings when the unfolding doesn't happen the way I prefer.

Humans are animals; we feel safer and less like prey when we are part of a pack and have a stockpile of what we think we need to survive. This had been the basis for my pursuit of happiness. So, when life stripped me of these two things (Brad as my pack and the company's client base as my safety net), I felt immensely unhappy. I'd had no warning, no time to find a new pack or gather a new stockpile. As I started taking beatings from the outside, my ego kicked into a dominant mindset of survival, and I began to react (taking action without adequate contemplation) to the threats I perceived. As I was nurturing my hurt and unhappy feelings, I was giving my *unconscious* mind the authority to lead me through my crisis. The *unconscious* mind operates from past data—what has been seen and experienced before—and influences thoughts and behavior from that perspective. This means I was relying on a storehouse of old data to navigate me out of something I'd never seen or experienced before.

This is the design of survival instincts. We all know the concept of touching a hot stove and instinctively (without thought) not touching it the next time. It is a quick response system, so if we are not locked in on controlling our survival instincts (operating consciously), we find ourselves reacting before realizing we are *re-acting* in moments that require new responses. We do this and wonder why we repeat history in our relationships, careers, finances, and emotions.

Going Back to Move Forward

The Universal Law of Compensation basically says that what we put out is what we get back. I eventually got this and learned how critically important it is to pause and allow myself to be present and conscious about my thoughts and actions. But to learn how to pause, I had to unlearn how to react and that required some major inner digging. I had to find my way to the root of why I had fallen into living so unconsciously (on autopilot). How, I asked myself, did I become so surrendering and willing to let the outside world control when I felt happy and when I did not? When did feeling safe (reacting as necessary to have a pack and a stockpile) become equivalent to being happy? Well, I asked the universe, and while meditating one morning, a childhood memory surfaced, and I got an answer.

I am a typical middle child, and I admit to having the middle child trait of feeling overshadowed. I believed growing up that I was much less significant in our household than my older and younger sisters. Most of what I did as a child and teenager I did on my own, feeling the people in my home had little interest in my life. It isn't that my parents and sisters didn't love me—I definitely felt their love. I just didn't feel the level of interest in me that I saw given to my sisters. I felt less important. I tucked this feeling away inside and found my own space. The good side of all of this is that I learned to be independent.

I grew up in Southeast Washington, DC, which was (and arguably remains) the roughest area of the city with the most violence and crime. The street I grew up on was a close-knit community of working families. Other than occasional home burglaries, we were pretty isolated from crime.

On the streets surrounding us, things were very different, which created a challenging elementary school experience for me. Most of the kids I went to school with lived where the crime mostly happened, and they brought that energy and way of life to school. My daily goal was to manage my way around after-school fights, which came with occasional knife threats. Some of the kids were in and out of juvenile detention, and though I didn't understand what I was seeing at the time, some were experiencing abuse at home. One of my worst experiences at that school was getting caught in an isolated area one day by a boy who should have been in middle school but had been kept back a couple of grade levels. He threatened to sexually assault me, but I somehow cried my way out of it.

I wasn't cut out for the environment, but to survive, I had to pretend I was. That was the only way I knew to safely get through my days. Acting like I was like them was my only form of protection. It was such an intense situation. Just looking in the wrong direction and catching the eye of the wrong person could create a lot of problems. In that school, bullying was not an incident; it was the culture.

The summer before fourth grade, my parents sat me and my two sisters down to tell us they'd made school changes. Hallelujah! The news was unexpected, and I can't describe the combination of joy and relief I felt.

My mom told us, "We found a really nice private school in Virginia. It's about an hour away, but the school has a bus service that we will use." My father proudly pulled out a few school brochures.

I quickly grabbed one. The school was beautiful, *and* it had horseback riding! This was beyond anything I could have imagined. I was actually going to a new school. Until that moment, I hadn't realized how much fear and sadness I had been carrying and suppressing inside. What I was hearing was more than good news.

My mom continued, "Melanie will start in the prekindergarten program, which isn't in the same building as Machell's sixth grade class."

"So, what building will I be in?" I asked.

My parents paused, and one of them said, "You won't be going there."

I was disappointed not to be going to the same school but still excited. Going to any place new was better than what I was leaving! "Where is my new school?"

My parents grew silent as if they hadn't anticipated this part of the conversation. My father hunched over a bit and softened his voice apologetically as he told me, "You won't be going to a new school—only Machell and Melanie."

About a month later, I watched as my older sister got dressed in her new uniform for the first day at her new school. The envy I felt exacerbated the anxiety I had about my own first day. I got dressed, and as I did every year, I prayed that some kids from the neighborhood would either not come back or at least not be in my class. I remained at that elementary school for another two years while my sisters went to their school in Virginia.

I was surprised that this childhood memory surfaced during my meditation. It is one I seemingly had locked away in my subconscious and hadn't thought about in many years, but the impact was clear. That was the first time I remember feeling insignificant, almost invisible. And it was a feeling that came from the people I viewed as loving me most. It was a major message that sank in as a subconscious thought I held about myself, and it played out in unconscious ways. Looking back, I know what my parents did was not intended to hurt me, just as I came to understand that Brad's decision to leave me alone in the company was not intended to hurt me. Neither decision was about me. Perhaps my parents could only afford two tuitions, and my name drew the short straw. But their decision caused collateral damage. What was that damage? My self-esteem. I internalized my parents' decision as a message that I wasn't their priority. This created a framework for self-ambivalence. There was a war inside me between thoughts of not being good enough or important enough (feelings of inferiority) and my primitive nature to self-preserve, which required me to promote and look out for myself. It was a pendulum swing, but my priority was safety. My posture had become to find a comfortable back seat and convince myself to be okay staying in it as long as it allowed me to have what I thought I needed to survive. This was a very unconscious strategy, but somehow, I figured out doing this could protect me physically and emotionally.

Each time Brad wanted the better parts of our world (in the business and at home), I let him. The permission I gave was a natural posture for me. I'd had many years of practice by the time we came together. It wasn't difficult for me to pose as Brad's employee, pass on the CEO title in the company, and stuff down the frustration of people believing the company belonged to him because I was used to modifying my self esteem to stay safe. Standing in the shadow is where I had all my practice; it was home base for me. I used Brad and the company to build a cocoon that felt safe, and I wanted to stay there.

As I said before, the reality was that long before the crisis of Brad's departure hit, I didn't even like the cocoon anymore. But the perception of comfort it gave me seemed worth the discomfort it required. I was not inspired inside this cocoon, and I certainly wasn't happy. I had no affinity for the work that was going on in it; nor was I proud of the self-honoring compromises I had to make to keep it together. Brad's departure forced a process of transformation that made it increasingly difficult for me to pretend I hadn't outgrown it.

My initial response to the reality of this transformation was to label everything as failures. I wanted to point to the business and say it was failing when it was simply changing. It was going through a natural process of growth that I didn't have the inspiration or commitment to lead it through. My marriage wasn't failing, either. It, too, was going through a needed transition to allow Brad and me to experience life from a different dynamic—one we never would have experienced staying locked in the small cocoon we had created together. I began to see how the pain, resistance, obstacles, victimhood, and ego struggles that were part of my existence were simply rooted in a fear of leaving our cocoon.

Ego Consciousness

I was once told there are two ways to view fear: *false evidence appearing real* or *f**k everything and run.*

My emotions at this juncture of self-awareness were overwhelming but too intense to shut off. My soft inner voice, beckoning me to live through inspired action, had gained volume but it was in direct opposition to a desire I still had to hold parts of my world together. The conflict between safety and happiness had me in a challenging space, and I struggled to consistently choose the signal I knew I should follow. I fought hard against the softer voice and continued to contort myself and distort reality until the universe sent me another experience to make sure I'd choose right.

My company was continuing to make progress, and we had secured several technology and other nonconference contracts. I was at an event one evening when a client introduced me to a CEO of a fast-growing IT company. The CEO asked me to come out to see his new office space; he wanted the two of us to chat about opportunities our companies could potentially partner on. He was super aggressive. I didn't know much about his company, but he seemed pretty well informed about mine. His energy was annoyingly eager (especially considering where my head was at the time). I didn't want to go to his office to meet with him, but I agreed to do it anyway.

I expected the meeting to be a preliminary discussion on ways our two companies might collaborate. I did nothing to prepare for it other than invite one of my vice presidents to attend. My intention was to have the two of *them* chat. I had neither the interest nor the energy to lead that discussion. I was only present in body as a courtesy to our mutual client.

We arrived at this CEO's new office space, and it didn't disappoint. It was beautiful. We were escorted to a conference room, and when I looked inside, my stomach sank. The room was jam-packed, and my name tent was at the head of the table. *Oh crap.* Fear, anxiety, anger, embarrassment. I was mentally checked out, consumed by all the new revelations I was having about myself and my life. This meeting was not close to being a priority. I slowly made my way to the head of the table.

The CEO jumped right into the meeting. He gave a flattering over-the-top introduction of me and my company. Meanwhile, my inner thoughts were calling me out: *Imposter!* Nothing he said felt like the truth. The CEO told the room full of salespeople staring at me that I was going to lead the way for our two companies to open a lot of doors and reap great profits. My thoughts stopped beating myself up and shifted to him. I was thinking, *Why are you doing this? You liar! Who are you?* Now I was pissed. How could I have gotten myself in this? I'd done it again. I had let my unconscious posture steamroll the opportunity I had to pause when he extended the invitation. That pause would have allowed me to give him a conscious answer that would have kept me out of the situation and that room. I was having this conversation in my head when I realized the CEO was gesturing for me to take control of the meeting and begin my *presentation.*

Of course, I had no presentation! I was so caught off guard that my mind went blank. I literally had no words. I stood up, now sweating in the hot, crowded room. I couldn't get my brain to cooperate so I could at least pretend I cared about partnering with them. I couldn't put one cohesive sentence together, not even one of the countless, brainless, on-the-spot pitches about my company I'd done thousands of times. I stood there with nothing. This was beyond brain fog. It was as if my spirit won the battle over my brain and refused to allow me to betray myself one more time. But this was not the time and place for that victory!

I stood there exposed. My masquerade ended in those seconds. I was so disconnected from everyone and everything in that room. Of course, I knew this before I agreed to the meeting, but only *I* knew it. The seconds felt like minutes. There we were, all jammed together wondering if as a pack we could help each other feel safer. The hope was palpable, as if what was inside that room could conquer what was outside it so we could each feel something inside that the outside could never permanently deliver. This was what I had come to understand, but it certainly wasn't what I could say in that moment. But I also couldn't betray myself.

So there was only one thing I could do. I thanked them for inviting me, picked up my things, and left. Silent confusion filled the room. As I walked out, my embarrassment and shame took over, unleashing horrendous mental lashings as I tried to put one step in front of the other. My vice president looked mortified, but I did not look back to see if he had followed me.

I barely reached my car before the tears started. Life was beating me up pretty good; I was at a point where I couldn't even fake it. I was no longer who I had been, and I was nowhere near comfortable with who I was becoming. Control of my world and my external composure had been my weapons of resilience, but not anymore. That meeting was the final sign. I didn't fit and didn't want to fit in the world I had created for myself. Like Brad figured out, I no longer wanted to be the CEO of my company. The company and I were undeniably incompatible.

The dictionary defines *ego* as "a person's sense of self-esteem or self-importance."[1] I contemplated this definition and realized just how much self-esteem was an Achilles' heel for me. I put up a good front, but deep inside, at levels that were easy to ignore, I had major self-esteem issues. When Brad left me at the company, these issues were triggered and made their way above the subconscious level where they'd been for many years.

A decade's worth of prayers I'd prayed before Brad left were pleas to be shown my purpose and feel fulfilled in life. I *said* I wanted to do meaningful, rewarding, and spirit-lifting work. Through the shift of my circumstances and transformation of my mindset, these prayers were being answered. The door was opened to make new choices and create a new reality. But to do this, I had to create a new me.

Every unwanted two-by-four lesson pushed me closer to the life I said I wanted. When I failed to do my part to voluntarily create what I said I wanted, the universe kindly stepped in to force my hand. I said I wanted purpose and joy, but I was committed to creating safety. The cocoon I was in wasn't built for my individuality, so it could never have given me the happiness I really wanted. I was living as a version of myself that was not serving the greater possible version of me. That was the real source of my pain—not Brad and not the changes in the company. Brad and the company were catalysts that simply forced me out.

I bartered to stay where I'd been until I didn't have enough left in me to trade. Funny, when Brad and I were first building the business, I slept soundly knowing we had mounting bills with just a few thousand (and sometimes just hundreds) in the bank. I felt purpose in building a company together for our family. Fast-forward two decades, after amassing decent wealth and more stuff than I needed, I often found myself praying for just a few hours of restful sleep. The purpose of creating a foundation for our family had been achieved, but I stayed until that purpose deteriorated into a transactional existence to sustain money. That wasn't living.

I once read that we give life to what we fear by giving that fear our attention, which in many ways, is a form of honoring that fear. The ego is a critical element to be aware of—it's important to be conscious of the role it plays in our thoughts and actions, especially if it is motivated by fear. The ego is the "I" we decide we are—our desires, our actions, our persona, and who we want others to believe we are. It creates our road map for belonging;

it evaluates what's happening outside us and affects our thoughts and feelings inside. When it isn't consciously managed, it can wreak havoc.

My ego had me convinced I needed to *save* the company, and if I did not, life as I had known it would fall apart—as if that would have been a bad thing. My ego sensed a threat of loss and stoked my emotions of fear. As a result, I could only think about holding everything together. It was at that point of reasoning that a shift in my mindset would have served me best. Operating in fear kept me fixated on Brad's return and obsessed with creating ways to circumvent any drop in the company's revenue. My ego blocked the universe's invitation for change. There was a beautiful new season unfolding, and there I was kicking and screaming, doing all I could to not move into it because it didn't look or feel like I expected.

Open-minded people position themselves to experience life beyond what they've known. Meaning, they are willing to release prior beliefs, plans, and goals in exchange for ideas and experiences they haven't yet conceived. I've thought about this extensively. The truth of this for me is that I am pretty open-minded in areas of my life that don't affect my safety and security. I can embrace new ways of seeing and doing things, even when these new ways come from people who see life very differently than I do. But I tend to resist and can be close-minded to accepting things that disrupt my personal comfort. The concept of this was not a huge *aha*, but seeing it in action once I became conscious of it was—like Brad's decision to move on. An open-minded person would have accepted long before I did that if Brad wanted to be in the company with me, he would have been. I had been super clear about what I wanted and what I thought was needed. He gave me an answer, but I had a fixed mind about the answer I wanted to hear.

Unconscious fear ("false evidence appearing real") will sometimes make us fight when we should celebrate being set free. It can make us miss out on greater happiness because we are afraid to let go of what we already have. The lifestyles of celebrities have always piqued my interest. They sell their personal freedom, live in seclusion, can't roam the world in peace, and many live in fear of losing their relevance, looks, and fame. I don't know how happy most of them are living that way but the point is: sometimes it is easy to start off with one goal and unconsciously imprison ourselves in lifestyles, relationships, dependencies, and beliefs that negate the joy of the achievement. Boxer Rubin "Hurricane" Carter once said, "Whatever I've done in life has led me to where I am today. Therefore, if I want to get out of prison and stay out of prison, I've got to turn around and go the other way."[2] We can't be afraid to turn the other way (when we have a choice, and we typically do) if the choices we've made aren't producing the experiences we desire.

Fear exists for good reasons; it helps us survive. But we need to be conscious about it. The voice of fear must drive us to be vigilant and not paranoid, cautious but not scared, and determined but not blind. Seeking safety and wanting acceptance are natural desires. But when the pursuit of those desires is out of balance, we can shift from healthy self-esteem to self-importance, from expressing individualism to division, and from disappointment to anger—and then we operate in dangerous spaces. This happened to me. My fears drove me to blast Brad with ugly attacks and attempts to dim his light. And when he didn't respond the way I wanted, fear made me turn those thoughts to myself.

To untether myself from the self I'd gotten cozy being, I had to thrust myself into taking risks that were unappealing. There seemed to be no gentle way to peel myself away. I had to start listening to the right voice inside me and tune out the raging, critical one that triggered my paranoia and kept my fears alive. I had to remind myself that fears were events that have not and possibly never would happen. Every imagined fear I held was just a blockage to every outcome I desired. The soft voice inside keeps me calm and hopeful—it feeds me rational, positive thoughts. This good voice, as I call it, gives me permission to reinvent myself in as many ways and as often as I choose. Listening to it became the single most important practice for me.

How do I do this? I set clear boundaries with myself. I say "*with* myself" and not "*for* myself" because somehow saying "for myself" feels akin to an old mindset of calculating and compromising based on too much external data. I practice purifying my thoughts before giving them permission to grow. Is the thought stoking unnecessary fear or is it offering a calm, new perspective? Is the thought creating more problems or is it moving me toward solutions? Will the thought result in division or cooperation?

The quiet time I spend each morning in my prayer room gives me the space to defeat any imbalance of my ego before it can get started in my day. In that time, before I face the forces out in the world, I remind myself who I choose to be, what is real and what is imagined, which lessons from my past serve me to remember, and which experiences I am better off forgetting.

This is how I live in the present moment with ego consciousness. I slow myself to recognize what I might be fearing in the moment that isn't yet real, I connect with my highest truth (who and how I choose to be in the absence of that fear), and I give myself permission to re-create my reality as I choose (untethered to who I've been or am expected to be).

PROVE IT LESSON

Ego is part of the human experience—it is always present. When it isn't balanced, it can stir thoughts of superiority or inferiority. Either extreme can cause us to make choices and behave in ways that can create distance between our external experiences and our innermost desires. The ego wants to protect the self, so it must assess how we are doing as compared to what is happening outside us. But too much outside-in focus can distort and overshadow our truth, individuality, and authenticity.

PROVE IT QUESTIONS

- How would I describe my ego—how is it showing up in my life?
- In what areas do I feel imposturous (unnatural) or "disturbable" (overly sensitive)?
- In what situations is my ego imbalanced (we all have these situations)? What are my typical thoughts and behaviors?

PROVE IT MINDFUL PRACTICES

When you feel imposturous (unnatural) or disturbed (discontent), write down the situations and people stirring that energy within you. What demands of the situation and traits of the people involved disturb you most? In a quiet space, allow yourself to sit in the energy (don't shoo it away) and then write down the feelings you experience—for example, judgment, shame, distrust, envy, and so on. Next, explore and write down what is inside you that is making you feel that way. Consciously work to eliminate the internal triggers you wrote down.

For the comprehensive PROVE IT Mindshifts Journaling Guide, please refer to the appendix.

CHAPTER 6

INSECURITY TO INNER PEACE

Transformation: the operation of changing (as by rotation or mapping) one configuration or expression into another
—MERRIAM-WEBSTER DICTIONARY

IT'S A BIG DECISION TO flip yourself inside out—that is, to release what everyone and everything outside you expects based on the persona you've molded and perfected for decades. This is especially true when you don't know what abandoning that persona and listening to your inner self will yield. Truthfully, had I been told and given time to think about the emotional fortitude doing this actually required, I might have chickened my way into protecting my old self. There were many times during my journey of "becoming" when reverting felt like an easier path. But as is typically the case, my thoughts about the journey were scarier than the journey itself. The mindset I was trying to leave behind was masterful at conjuring up worst-case scenarios, subconsciously giving power to worries about what could go wrong and what I could lose. Inevitably, nothing that ever went wrong or I ever lost was catastrophic. In fact, the losses often turned out to be an emancipation from commitments blocking my way forward.

Learning to Be Comfortable Being Uncomfortable

I am far from perfect in the practice of staying true to myself. It is difficult to do in a world that thrives on selling us thoughts about who we should be, how we should think, and what we should look like. The endless saturation of messaging is hard to escape. As if the media isn't enough, we now have a parade of "influencers" flooding our screens to convince us of the what, where, and how to do life. These messages sink in and affect the paths we choose. And once we are on a path, the pressure to not veer from it—and disappoint those who either expect or need us to stay the course—can be enough to betray any inner calling to exit. It takes conscious commitment to choose life from your inner calling, especially after you've spent a lifetime carving out an existence that might be far from it.

Of course, detaching myself from the persona and roles that had defined me was a counterintuitive process. I had to learn to walk in the world again, unfamiliar with how to place one foot in front of the other in my new state of mind. I had to recognize subconscious thoughts and fight unconscious habits to clear space for more conscious decisions.

The road map for success I'd followed, mostly prescribed by outside demands and influences, hadn't landed me in a good place. Keeping this understanding in my conscious mind helped me push through the discomfort of shifting away from a life of predictability and safety. I felt pretty naked, and in the middle of this process, I still did not yet feel free. Actually, I felt like I was free falling—making up my life one day at a time, which felt crazy at my age. On any given day, I felt terror, disorientation, *and* exhilaration.

I'd seen countless movies about some character leaving behind a stable life to "find themselves," and now I was living it. I felt like I was watching myself from outside my own body. At this point on my journey of transformation, I was still physically running the business. I had commitments that demanded the old me to show up in the office. Managing the dichotomy between the two versions of me was a mental test. Malitta the expert contortionist wrestled daily with Malitta the enlightened because Malitta the enlightened was only interested in figuring out how to get free—the future of the company was not her priority.

The months that followed the uncomfortable CEO meeting I walked out of were an awkward time for me in my own company. The realization that I no longer wanted to be CEO made it difficult for me to show up and to be and do what the business needed. I became even more quiet and aloof than before, and I offered explanation to no one. I was too insecure about what my truth would sound like. I was in the middle of figuring myself out and couldn't afford to be asked any questions—at least not from anyone without a license to help me. The only thing I was sure of was the decision to get out of what I had gotten myself into.

An important step in that direction was to unlearn the habit of contorting. From childhood, it had been an autonomic response. For example, I quietly accepted my parents' decision to send me back to my elementary school. I held in the disappointment and pain, and I did what I "had to do" to survive it. But I should have thrown a hissy fit—right there in the middle of the kitchen floor so they could all see what I felt. Even if there was nothing they could have done about it, they would have at least been clear. Likewise, my reaction to Brad's departure wasn't much different. I stayed in the company and did what I "had to do," despite how much I didn't want to. I threw a hissy fit with him that day in my office, but I should have beaten him to the door and walked out first!

My habit of contorting was a response to insecurity. I became willing to sell my truer self to protect myself. As a child, it was for love and acceptance. As an adult, it was for money and success. Contorting should not be confused with compromise. Compromise involves mutuality, a situation where shared acceptance is involved. Compromise can create good energy. Contortion can create resentment.

> **Contorting should not be confused with compromise. Compromise can create good energy. Contortion can create resentment.**

As I reflected on all of this, it was easy to see how I had contorted in the business—conceding on professional titles, playing second fiddle, and so on. I did not have the grounds to be angry with Brad about it. I chose to do it and labeled it sacrifice. But had I also done this in my marriage? Had I sold off parts of myself (contortion not compromise) in my relationship with Brad? Of course I had! The company and our marriage were too intertwined for this not to have been true. No wonder he felt comfortable walking out. Why wouldn't he have? I'd been an expert contortionist, and I think he was confident that I would contort just a little more to cover him and carry the business in his absence. And I did!

Contorting remained my go-to posture until I'd twisted myself into such a state of resentment that any form of happiness was far from my reality. I had let my insecurities and fears trap me in a bad place. There was an ever-present energy of sadness in my life, and as I began to see and understand myself, it became increasingly difficult to suppress it. My first response was to blame the people and world around me for my sadness, but that was neither true nor helpful. As I said, no one but me was responsible for my choices. I was faced with this question: Could I give my inner self the same level of reverence I'd given the outside world? Could I honor my most authentic self regardless of what it might cost me? Not just for a day but for every tomorrow I have left?

Inner Peace

Watching Brad was an interesting lesson. As I've mentioned, I was at first convinced that his decision to leave the company had been completely selfish. And it was—that was the part I focused on. But as I opened my mind about it all, I had to consider (reluctantly) another perspective. Maybe he'd gotten to the very same place I'd just arrived. Maybe he could no longer perpetrate and contort, selling his dreams and desires to amass profits doing work that neither inspired nor fulfilled him. I didn't want to, but I had to sit with this possibility. At this point, I thought I'd mostly forgiven Brad, but I realized I hadn't. I was still looking at him through a lens of resentment, unwilling to consider anything positive in what he'd done. It's funny, what we can see so clearly in others is sometimes the very thing we don't recognize in ourselves. I had been pretty selfish through the entire experience, but that never crossed my mind. I had been too focused on my needs and "sacrifice." But when I considered the possibility that Brad had done what I was now struggling to do for myself, I saw someone who looked a little more like the man I married, the one I respected. Brad was seeking his own path from within, something he had tried to explain to me over and again, but I was too fearful and heartbroken to hear what he was saying. Each time I felt he was betraying me, was he really just trying not to betray himself? He never asked me to stay; he just said he wasn't coming back.

    Brad had watched me fight to save the company, and his silence should have been my invitation to let it go. When he walked out of the house the night I told him the news about the rescinded $17 million contract, he reinforced the message that the company simply wasn't important to him anymore. And when he chose, despite my pleas, to not come back to the company, I should have accepted that what we once had as business partners was over. He'd let it go. He needed to leave, and now, so did I.

As I began to incorporate this new mindset, my ego was challenged. I wanted so badly to shift into a better existence, but I struggled with putting my pride, reputation, and our prosperity on the line. Life was showing me the answer, and it was challenging me to put all my chips on the table. As the last one standing in the company (again, I should have beaten Brad to the door), I had a much harder decision to make. I felt my decision—not his—was the one jeopardizing our lifestyle and future. I devoured books and articles about midlife crises, hoping that one would shake me out of the notion of walking out on the *good* life I'd built. After all, supposedly I'd made it. I had success—why would I throw that all away? I must have said this to myself a million times. But saying it didn't make it true. Success is having a life you want to run to, not away from.

This realization was an interesting boomerang experience. In the 1990s, a friend gave me a ticket to *The Oprah Winfrey Show*—a big deal back then. The show was about women stepping out to start their own businesses. During the show, Oprah made a point of encouraging women to believe in themselves enough to step out and do what they love. My interpretation of what she was saying was to not worry about the money, that money will follow when passion leads. At the time, Brad and I were fully immersed in the struggle to get our business off the ground, short on money, and under pressure to make our dream work. So her message about money and passion irritated me. I knew that Oprah ended each show by shaking the hand of every person in her audience, and I couldn't wait for my turn. When she graciously shook my hand, I said, "How could you say something like that?" She looked completely confused. "How could you encourage people to just quit their jobs and recklessly pursue their passion—how are they supposed to keep their lights on?"

Oprah continued to be gracious. "Thank you for coming," she responded and kept things moving. (I'm still embarrassed.)

Fast-forward more than twenty years later, as I worked through my crisis, and Oprah's words made sense to me. I had better inner peace when I was worried about keeping my lights turned on than I did at the height of my company's success. That's the problem with filling life up with work without passion. Had I created a situation of work that allowed me to incorporate passion (even if I needed to do this outside my daytime work), I doubt the emptiness I experienced would have been so intense. Instead, I filled my work life to the brim with what felt like work. This was a performance of contortion for the reward of compensation. But eventually, the compensation couldn't medicate the pain.

Vocation (what we do to support ourselves) and passion (feeling energized and excited about what we do) can often remain mutually exclusive, depending on circumstances. When this is the case, there can be a challenge of one consuming so much time and energy that it overshadows and leaves little to no space for the other to exist.

I pushed myself to live with the emptiness I felt as my vocation consumed my life. It didn't work. So I stopped running from it, slowed my days, and learned to do more observing than moving. I became more familiar with the parts of me I liked and the parts of me I disliked. I was conscious about the possible mistake of dismantling my life only to incorporate back in parts of me I needed to get away from.

As my mindset shifts were happening, I became more aware of isolated moments of self-betrayal—those small moments that seem harmless but further immerse me in commitments and roles I don't want. I learned to protect myself and as I did, the people around me (including Brad) struggled to find a new balance and rhythm with me. I had changed my rules of engagement, and they were no longer sure what box to put me in. They couldn't affect how I was showing up. I needed the space (box free) to put enough distance between my thoughts and my choices, allowing my*self* to design how I would align with the outside world (inside out and not the other way around).

Giving too much consideration to what was happening outside me had been my prison. To break free, I didn't become selfish, but I did become more self-kind. It is an interesting experience to strip away (as much as you can) the many opinions of yourself you pick up and incorporate in a lifetime and then try and define for yourself, who you are. When we are brave enough to search and honest enough to acknowledge, we are the ones who know ourselves best.

During the time I took the journey within myself, I endured quite a bit of scrutiny, particularly from professional colleagues. My quiet and more observant demeanor didn't feel or look much like the high-energy, demanding, chaser of success everyone had gotten comfortable with. I was much more contemplative and slower to move, and it made people uncomfortable. There were days I could feel them questioning my ability to lead, but giving any energy to that would have compromised my inner compass. I was fighting an important war, and it required me to focus more on what I wanted and less on what I did not. I had to silence the voices that were not leading me to what I was seeking.

So I shrank my world as much as I could, avoiding people and commitments moving in the opposite direction of where I wanted to go. This was my strategy to control those automatic behaviors and responses that had caused the schism between my more authentic self and my persona that the world and I had created. In time, and after much practice, I grew less inclined to explain myself or make excuses for not being who my world expected. Realigning my commitments and obligations to reduce internal contradiction became a priority. I recall one of my executives implying, through questions that weren't very subtle, that perhaps I was having some sort of breakdown. I smiled to myself because in many ways I was, and I was grateful.

Keeping a safe space to develop and nurture a new mindset was the only protection I had. The work in the company was still demanding, and I still had an overload of responsibilities. Mixing in the thoughts, expectations, and needs of others before being clear about my own had been part of the imprisoned life that had gotten me off course. Within the safe space I began to build for myself, I could pause. And after pausing, I could choose and respond from a conscious place and do a better job of aligning my inner feelings, thoughts, and desires with my external commitments and responsibilities.

Shifting to conscious living means shifting away from unconscious assimilation. Assimilation is natural. Life is designed for coexistence, so naturally we conform and adopt habits, attitudes, and beliefs to fit in. But when we do this out of order, assimilate without first being clear about who we choose to be and how we choose to experience life, we find ourselves in a position of struggle because we have not consciously chosen who, what, and how to align external influences along our journey. Once I got clearer about this, my priorities and focus flipped to a posture of honoring and trusting (not fighting) that calm, quiet voice inside. It is the key and road map in life and it's always there.

I had to work to recognize and develop trust in this voice. It is so much softer and gentler than the loud, pushy voice I'd been accustomed to. I gravitated to teachings by experts like Caroline Myss, Kute Blackson, Panache Desai, Michael Beckwith, Neale Donald Walsch, and so many others. I hold gratitude for their guidance on balancing the mental, physical, and energy parts of who I am. I stopped going to business symposiums and started attending woo-woo self-transformation conferences. I left those woo-woo experiences more equipped, liberated, and clear than I ever was after any of the many executive courses and business conferences I've spent thousands of dollars on. This is because the woo-woo conferences taught me to focus on who I am being and then concern myself with what I am doing. That is something none of the business courses or conferences had done for me.

I shifted to prioritizing contentment above money. How did this shift align with my desire (and fears) to sustain and not have to adjust my lifestyle? It didn't fully. Again, I had to trust myself, and I also had to be willing to risk losing it all. My contentment was that important to me. I still held the responsibility of serving as CEO, and those responsibilities were important to me as well. The goal was to minimize the intrusion of my work responsibilities on my peace. I took a few simple steps. Here's an example. It was trendy for "progressive" CEOs to maintain an open-door policy—something I never actually liked but did anyway. As part of my transformation to better inside-out living, I simply stopped leaving my office door open. I felt I had to protect my personal space so I could maintain the practice of re-*minding* myself. I decided my office would no longer be a place for a variety of energies to come and go throughout my day. I started conducting most of my interactions in a neutral place, not in the space I needed to protect.

The more I took actions like this and became less accessible and in the middle of everyone else's firestorms, the more Brad's name resurfaced. For some, he had become a legendary hero they greatly missed. They seemed to forget that he'd been the one who left them. When I was no longer being and doing what they wanted, they (like I once had) turned their sights back to Brad, hoping he would come back and get things back to "normal." The old Malitta would have cared.

Inner peace expanded as I became more and more comfortable leveraging the power of "no." I trained myself to tip the scales away from concerns about how my choices affected others, so I could lean in more consciously about how my choices were affecting me. Sounds selfish? I agree. It wasn't a posture I planned to keep forever, but it was necessary in this season of transformation. Had I not allowed myself to be intentionally selfish about my time, thoughts, and responses, I'd likely still be in the loop of unconsciously creating inner discord. I had to reconcile where I was with where I wanted to be, and this could only happen if the world's opinions were limited enough for me to form my own.

I learned that the body is an amazing compass and unlike the mind, its signals are unfiltered. The body can guide the mind toward truths. I had been living in reverse, allowing my mind to trigger my body, many times with imagined truths. My mind told me Brad had abandoned me, so my body felt sick and sad about his abandonment. My mind told me the company was under a grave threat, so my body felt high anxiety and worry in dealing with it. If instead I had taken the lead from my body, I might have felt Brad's love despite his decision to leave the company. Had I allowed my body to lead as I dealt with the future of the business, I might not have taken actions I labeled as preventive but proved to be unnecessary knee jerks to imagined scenarios that did not yet exist. The body senses real danger, the mind sometimes only imagines it.

It was an amazing behavior shift to start listening to my body. Doing this has saved me repeatedly. When my body senses negative energy in a situation or with someone, I pause long enough to consciously decide how I would like to adjust or distance myself. My body gave me a signal the night my client introduced me to that CEO whose office I dashed out of, but I didn't listen. I dismissed the signal as a lack of enthusiasm on my part rationalizing in my mind that I didn't want to do the meeting because I was feeling disengaged. My body sensed the disconnection between our energies, but I let my mind override that sensation. My mind told me what I should do (respectfully honor his request to meet), and my body was telling me what was best to do (decline).

It was my small triumphs in moving away from who I had been that paved the way for larger ones taking me closer to where I wanted to be. The more I showed up consciously aligning my thoughts and actions in each present moment, the better I got at forgetting who others expected me to be. It was liberating. I didn't know from one day to the next who Malitta would become—that's what I call living. I shed the many layers and years of her persona and allowed her to be consciously re-created from a place of inner peace not fear.

I was struck by my progress when riding in an Uber one day with my mom and Brad on the way to a funeral in New York City. While riding, I got a call from the chairperson of a nonprofit board I was on at the time. My mom was listening as the chair asked me to double the already generous annual donation I had committed to making. She wanted me to announce my double contribution during an upcoming gala and challenge the audience to follow my lead. The old Malitta, whether I would have wanted to or not, would have gracefully responded without much thought and agreed to do it (especially with my mom listening). But as soon as she asked, I felt a sickness in my stomach. The new Malitta knew better. I had been struggling with my alignment with this nonprofit and was actually contemplating stepping down from the board. A commitment to double my contribution would have been a double betrayal to myself. And worse yet, it would have required me to live out that betrayal publicly.

I gave the chair a conscious and aligned response: "No, I won't be able to do that." And I said nothing more. The chair was perplexed and scrambled for something to say as I remained silent. She began to apologize, assuming my reason for turning down the request was financial. It was not, but I offered no further explanation (another gift of growth to myself). I refused to allow her perception to prompt me to explain and justify my decision. Honoring myself shouldn't require excuses. I was continuing to become someone I liked.

By the time I reached this point in my journey, it had been about three and a half years since Brad left the company. I was working in my office one afternoon when someone knocked on my office door. To my surprise, it was Brad. I couldn't remember the last time he'd been in the office during the workday. We'd landed in a better space at home and had moved past the volatility. I assumed he was surprising me to take me to lunch.

He smiled and said, "Hey, I'm ready to come back."

PROVE IT LESSON

Relying too much on external confirmation about who we are and how we are doing can create insecurities and inner conflict. Wanting to assimilate is natural, but it is important to first be clear about what you want to experience (not have) and who you choose to be (not do) in the process. The body can help you define the answers; it doesn't lie. Remember to pause, listen, and give your mind time to process its signals. Use the body's language of energy as a compass.

PROVE IT QUESTIONS

- In what area of my life am I discontented and why?
- What role are external influences playing in my experience of discontent?
- Is there something I can do to lessen my reliance on external cues and influences and expand inner peace?

PROVE IT MINDFUL PRACTICES

Spend quiet time reflecting on areas that are causing discontent. As you think about these areas, notice the responses and signals from your body. Describe the signals in your journal and then contemplate reasons why you're having those sensations. Decide how you should adjust or eliminate your choices to create better contentment.

For the comprehensive PROVE IT Mindshifts Journaling Guide, please refer to the appendix.

CHAPTER 7

TIP OF THE ICEBERG TO TOP OF THE MOUNTAIN

> What steps do you normally take when you get serious about doing something differently? You separate yourself . . . and you begin to plan a course of action related to the new self.
> —JOE DISPENZA, *BREAKING THE HABIT OF BEING YOURSELF*

WHEN A LARGE PIECE OF a glacier breaks off and is carried out to sea, it becomes an iceberg that drifts with the currents of the ocean, with about only one-eighth of it being visible above water.

This is a good metaphor for the way I had lived. The world was only getting a fraction of the person I was inside, and I'd become comfortable with that arrangement. It felt safe. But the unexpected shifts that shook my foundation left me no other choice than to evolve.

The process of breaking the habits I developed living as an iceberg took about three years. One of those three years was spent dealing with emotional shock and trepidations in isolation. During that year, I held on to pain and resisted how my life was falling apart in what felt like fast motion. Year two was when I began to face my fears and release my vice grip on what had been, realizing I needed to examine and reengineer my perspective and my actions. And in year three, I faced the real problem—I had contorted myself into a way of life and a situation that I didn't want to be in. Had I continued to live in pain, resist inner truths, see nothing but obstacles, and live like a victim (i.e., decided not to PROVE IT), I would have remained an iceberg, drifting with the currents around me, giving the world and experiencing only a fraction of who I am. My cries and prayers to the universe to live with purpose and have better peace and contentment were answered. The initial answers to my prayer felt like a punishment, but as I pushed through each answer, I was led to a more rewarding path.

My old mindset could not process the blessing of Brad's departure. It was fixed on having things one way, and when that one way dissipated, my unconscious and immediate response was anger and sadness. Thoughts of betrayal and injustice were triggered by my fears and I never paused long enough during those initial miserable months to give conscious consideration to what was happening. Had I paused, I could have saved us both a lot of suffering. The contorting I'd done to support the company's success had been weighing me down for years, long before Brad decided to leave. I didn't recognize the doorway that was right in front of me when Brad let the business go because I was too busy reacting to the pain I imagined he was inflicting on me. My unconscious mind had been the master; it took control when I sensed a threat to my existence, and I not only allowed it but fed it by trying to keep things as they had been. In my fixed mindset, there was only one acceptable outcome.

Brad and I were supposed to grow our business together into an empire that would live beyond us. That is the dream we had when we started and a vow we both committed to keep. But we were young. We had no idea how much living out your dream can change your feelings about it. When Brad left, my dream hadn't yet fully changed. I wanted more purpose and contentment from my work (the part of the dream the company was not doing for me), but I also wanted to hold onto my wealth (the part of the dream the company was giving me). Building wealth and doing it with Brad were the parts of my cocoon I was initially fighting to keep.

I was mislabeling my life in that cocoon as success. I bought what I wanted and created a lifestyle to convince myself there was joy for me living in it. Even after Brad and the company outgrew the cocoon, I was willing to stay in there trying to hold it together. The truth is, as you know by now, I was committed to being comfortable, and that required Brad and the company to stay in place. It was a mindset that blocked me from dreaming a new dream. I didn't want to walk away from my *good* life. But shouldn't a good life *feel* good?

When Brad came to my office that afternoon, telling me he wanted to return to the company, he was a different person than the one who had left, and so was I. It was a chance to reset. We discussed what a return would look like. Where did we want to take the company? How did we want to coexist? There was a lot to figure out. We weren't in our twenties this time. We had both seen, lived through, and become what we never imagined. The one thing we quickly agreed on was making choices about our future based on being happy, which meant not re-creating the past.

One day, during the weeks Brad and I continued to talk about what happiness would look like for us, I came across the Facebook profile of a childhood friend. I looked at her smile and felt a fluttering sensation in my heart: envy. I told myself that anyone could look happy on Facebook, but her smile looked so genuine. Growing up, she'd always had the best laugh, the kind that makes everyone laugh just by hearing it. I reached out to her on Facebook to say hello, and a few days later, we connected by phone. She told me she never moved away from the neighborhood and described a simple life. She seemed to have enough to get by. She was happy and content, and I was definitely envious.

Walking the Walk

The reality of my past decisions had come full circle. I hadn't pursued happiness; Brad and I started with that as our goal, but in the end, we had pursued money and success. No wonder we ended up as we did. The work we fell into in the business carried no significance to either of us, and so neither of us carried any sustainable passion for it. The only real attachment was to what it generated to make us feel secure and accomplished. As I said before, most of us are pushed and prodded to not be average—to make it to the top with the assurance that the rewards are better there. But no one is average until they are herded into average behaviors. Each one of us is born uniquely with individual traits that can't be duplicated. It's as if we are taught early on to stifle individuality only later to be told to stand out. What if, I thought, I'd never left the person I was uniquely designed to be behind? What if I had been encouraged to shine in my own way, even if that meant looking less than average to the outside world? What if I never felt a need to stifle, contort, or conform the beauty of who I am inside to make everyone else be okay with me? Then, I thought, I never would have become an iceberg, sharing only a fraction of my true, one-of-a-kind self.

Life doesn't allow us to undo what we've experienced, but it does allow us to recalibrate our thoughts and start over. The first mindful decision I had to make to start over was to be excited about it. I had to fully release what was behind me and consider the past a gift that came for a season to lead me into a better one. I had to let the past go.

Brad and I would sit in our conference room, writing ideas and dreams about the next phase of us on a whiteboard. It really was déjà vu as we explored who and how we wanted to be with no particular answers. Only this time we were wise enough to incorporate who and how we didn't want to be. We talked about selling the company, but understanding the length and headache of that process, we decided against it. Instead, we agreed we should sell our most lucrative contracts and use the profits to give us a comfortable financial runway to be deliberate about our future.

We sold the contracts we identified quicker than we expected, and we kept select smaller ones that would keep a manageable level of operations (and revenue flow) in place. But there was one glitch in our plan. We were still in our office lease, the one I had tried unsuccessfully to get us out of after our second layoff. The monthly expense was an unnecessary cash burden we needed to eliminate. Our workforce was down to about a tenth of what it had once been. So the space had become even more of a financial and psychological burden. It was depressing for me and for Brad. It kept the past in the present and we wanted to shake it and move on.

Brad and I had both dealt with the landlord over the years. He was a major roadblock. So we had talked ourselves into staying through the remainder of the lease but were challenged on how to reconfigure everything for a much smaller company. I shared this dilemma with my life coach (I had gotten smart enough to engage and use a coach). My coach was great at piercing through camouflaged emotions, exposing blind spots, and pointing out nonsense. She asked a simple question: "If you don't want to be there *and* it isn't good for you to be there, why are you still there?"

Of course, I jumped in describing the landlord and my prior attempt to negotiate. She asked, "How do you know what's possible now?"

"Because before, when I—"

"Hold tight, I'm asking about now?"

"Okay, okay, I hear you."

The entire rent situation was an area of discomfort for me. It represented painful memories, and I conveniently labeled it an obstacle, which gave me the excuse to work around it and not through it. Besides, I preferred to avoid the landlord altogether.

Getting a life coach had been one of my better decisions. After that session, Brad and I laughed at the thought of trying to get the landlord to release us from our lease, but we laughed even more about not having tried again. We agreed to look at new space options before approaching him. Our son suggested we look at shared office space. At the time, this was a fairly new trend, and it was looked down on by "established" companies. Brad and I were more than opposed to the idea. (Another example of having a fixed mindset.) We were from a generation where the size and location of your office was a direct representation of your success (COVID completed the dismantling of that!). Moving from an entire floor of space with two large conference rooms, two kitchens, a private executive office suite, more than twenty-five private offices, and a lot of cubicles to a shared space that would require Brad and me to be in the same office seemed ridiculous. Our pride shut this idea down with a firm no.

Eventually, our son convinced us to just go and see for ourselves. We went and reluctantly admitted that it made great sense for us. Brad and I were unsure about where we wanted to take what was left of the company, if any place at all, so signing a new long-term lease (on top of the expensive lease we hadn't gotten out of) was not an option. We felt energized as we stood in the middle of a beautiful, shared office space in downtown Washington, DC. The space was located one block from a subway stop and only required a month-to-month lease. It would cost about 40 percent of what we were paying for our space in the suburbs. I was almost giddy.

The shared office space was bustling with entrepreneurs from different industries, sharing, exchanging, and collaborating in the open and relaxed common areas. There was enthusiasm and passion I hadn't felt in many years. It was clear our son had found the environment we needed. Our pride was going to have to take a back seat. We made the decision to move, which meant facing a confrontation with our existing landlord. We expected an ugly fight, but within two months, we were moving into our new, shared space. The landlord simply let us go. Brad and I still shake our heads in amazement about how that situation worked out, but when you make up your mind and take right action, the universe conspires on your behalf and miracles can happen.

Being set free from that lease was an important step forward for us, but the two-month process of moving and leaving our old life behind was much more emotional than I expected. As we packed up our old space, I felt I was packing up a chunk of my life and putting it in taped boxes. I was confronted with bad past emotions, including fear. I had no idea where we were going to take the company. But I was grateful to not be deciding alone. We boxed up remnants of our years together as husband and wife and business partners and struggled to toss out more than we kept. Brad and I worked together in that old office space late weeknights and weekend after weekend, purging and making decisions. It was a painful parting of ways. We had to reduce our life's work to what could fit in a five-office, already furnished, shared space. I cried often. There is a quote commonly attributed to Lao Tzu that says new beginnings can often be disguised as painful endings.

On good days, Brad and I locked arms and held on to good thoughts and memories. On bad days, the emotional toil of purging triggered low thoughts and bad energy. Those days were the toughest. I had to fight hard against resentment and victimhood. I wanted to feel sorry for myself and resist feeling happy to move forward. I felt entitled to feel pain and wanted Brad to own it. Again, this happened on my low days. The point is, low days will happen, but fortunately, with time, those moments grow to be more rare than common. I had to mindfully practice keeping thoughts that gave me good and not low energy, like envisioning our days in the new space in the middle of downtown Washington, DC, and not the rooms full of stuff we needed to throw away. We got through it, and in the end, we cleared the old space and moved on.

After a few weeks in our new space, the sting of what we put behind us lessened. We were in a good situation and free to reset and redefine our future. The reduced burden of operations and financial commitments allowed us the mental space we needed to meaningfully focus on the possibilities ahead. The planning process became fun. We worked from our new definition of success. For us, success meant feeling good about our work, commitments, and contributions while maintaining a pleasurable lifestyle. When we built our company two decades earlier, we had to integrate our ideas of success with the need to pay our bills. In this new season, we were freer to explore mission-driven work aligned with our individual definitions of purpose and joy, understanding that, if necessary, we had to be willing to let each other go in our own direction to make that happen.

As for the portion of the business that remained, we kept a small team of staff and allowed operations to run mostly without us. As Brad and I bounced around, exploring several different avenues, we tested a myriad of ideas. Some of those ideas were simply bad. Brad and I had been spoiled in the sense that we weren't going into this season willing to completely start at the bottom (grinding as hard as we had the first time to build up). So we tried a couple of shortcuts that didn't turn out to be a good idea. There was one in particular that made this lesson clear.

Brad led several significant health care initiatives during his time away from the business and developed a passion for health equity. I'd always had a passion for lifting marginalized communities. There was a new program launched by the federal government to help older adults with multiple chronic conditions manage their health to have a better quality of life. Beautiful—it brought our two passions together and we had the resources to hire a clinical team and build the technology. But rather than pursue this opportunity slowly, Brad and I agreed to partner with a group that promised accelerated growth using its existing network of doctors. Disaster. We spent nearly a year working with that group despite having no shared values, vision, or trust. We lost money and time and certainly didn't have a fulfilling experience.

Lesson learned. The journey into our new season wasn't going to be as cozy as we wanted. We were going to have to put more skin in the game (get our hands dirty). Our pride and pockets could not be the priority within the context of our agreed-on definition of success. We cut our losses on that chronic care project and got back on the path of conscious and more mindful decision-making. We fought against the anxiety of not knowing exactly where we were heading, and at our age there was nothing exciting about that. We were too young to stop working but old enough to not want to work as hard as we had before. But this period of time turned out to be important. We were forced to be more still and trust our inner compasses. During this period, I got better at honoring my best thoughts (ones rooted in wisdom and not fear) and began to create better experiences.

I was very clear about what my drift with the masses to *acquire* the masses' definition of success had done. It had me focused on what was outside me, when what I wanted was for the stuff inside me to be expressed in ways that could influence and lift others. That is where the seeds for my success resided. From this place, I create uniquely and beautifully from my authentic soul. It doesn't matter if I am volunteering at a shelter, coaching and supporting leaders, or even writing a book; each experience allows me to be an inspiration, spread positive energy, and share my joy. That makes me feel successful.

Living out our individuality is so commonly beaten out of us by the world that when someone happens to break through the entrapment of conformity, we label them as unique, a special talent, or even a celebrity. These are the people the highest rewards (money and applause) are often reserved for. But every human and every form of life is unique, has a special talent, and is qualified to be celebrated. As an iceberg, I didn't live as though this was true and the most beautiful and powerful parts of me were submerged and hidden. I thought the day Brad walked out was a shattering point in my life, but it was what broke me loose.

I had been praying endlessly for God to show up and grant me a miracle to protect my little world. I wanted some miraculous and magnanimous answer to swoop in so I could stay safely stuck in a situation and circumstance that was too small for what was inside me.

No miracle was coming because it had already arrived.

The miracle was in operation; I couldn't see it. It kept squeezing me to get my attention so I could transform and shift my mindset to seeing how *I* could create the life I wanted. This squeezing didn't just happen in my relationship with Brad and inside the business; it was happening in almost every area and relationship in my life. In fact, some of those other areas were the most uncomfortable. When things (like my identity and persona) began to change, I couldn't hold up a billboard to announce to everyone what was happening; nor did I feel comfortable trying to explain myself. The space I was in was so awkward that I mostly avoided social circles and spent a lot of time at home.

But one experience helped me break free. Brad and I were invited to a friend's house for a holiday gathering and reluctantly accepted. The invitation stated that wine was an "unnecessary" but appreciated gesture—which meant, among this particular group of friends, that a nice, expensive bottle of wine was expected.

Brad and I were pretty deep into practicing mindfulness and making conscious choices, and we had gotten pretty good at calling each other out—holding each other accountable. One area of accountability and mindful practice we agreed on was to stop overspending and being wasteful. Brad and I spent money mindlessly for years—too much to even estimate. We refused to go back to that way of life. We honored our commitment in large and simple ways, shifting away from eating out seven days a week to only on the weekends and refusing to buy ridiculously priced designer items and fine bottles of wine that to us didn't taste that much better than lesser priced wines.

We chatted about the wine expectation for the holiday party and initially agreed this was a "special" occasion and reason enough to override our conscious consumption commitment. But as the party date approached, neither of us felt good about our decision to break our rule. We admitted it: We were making a chicken move to avoid looking cheap. So we stuck with our values and bought a wine we had come to enjoy. We knew our friends would recognize the brand and therefore know the bottle had only cost about $12.

As we entered the party, the host greeted us and glanced down at our "unnecessary" gesture. I felt a flush of heat run through me, and I wanted so badly to take back our decision. Brad handed over the bottle and kept walking. I stood there watching the host clock the label, and I immediately absorbed judgment and disapproval. She tried to deliver a polite and gracious smile, but it was too late. Her body and my body had already communicated. She seemed to feel insulted, and I felt embarrassed. The loudmouth voice in me started beating me up in those long seconds as I took off my coat.

But just when that voice was about to win and ruin my night, I caught a glimpse of the host smirking and flashing our bottle in the direction of her friend as she took it to the kitchen instead of displaying it with the others. That snapped me back to my senses. She wasn't my friend; a friend would never do that. And why would I care about the opinion of someone who doesn't care about my feelings? I caught it, and I caught myself! Had I not seen what she did, I might have betrayed myself by either giving her some lame excuse or attempting to explain my journey (a confession the situation didn't deserve). The scenario was comical—I was experiencing in real time another attempt by my outer world to coerce me to fit in. I chuckled to myself and moved on to greet the other guests. Being conscious in that growth moment felt good.

That bottle of wine represented the new me. Neither I nor it fit in that night. My only regret is that I did not take the bottle back home with us. What sometimes looks like a lot really requires a little, and what sometimes looks like a little requires a lot. Taking a $150 bottle of wine to the party would have been a lot easier than the right choice: living in our truth. The $12 bottle, in our opinion, was just fine—especially since it was our *gesture* to make.

Shifting to My Mountaintop

A mountaintop experience is a moment of transcendence. I figured it out: I don't need to make sense to the world; the world needs to make sense to me.

Remember, there is a big difference between contorting and compromise. Compromise is something that is mutual and doesn't typically cause inner disturbances and lingering dis-*ease*. My iceberg existence was not a result of compromise. It happened after years of contorting to hold together the life I thought I was supposed to have. In many ways, it was an easier and cowardly decision. I was telling God, the universe, and anyone who would listen that I was unfulfilled, yet I was unwilling to let go of what was causing it.

When I think of a mountaintop, I think of peace and freedom. I imagine seeing beauty unencumbered by obstructions and distractions, far beyond the one place where I'm standing. On the mountaintop, I live from within, honor my intuition, express my creativity, and fully use my physical senses to experience life. I sat in the CEO seat of my company as an iceberg. After eventually completely releasing the business and emerging from that experience, I discovered and created success: I love being a coach, speaker, and author. I am content with my commitments. I make valuable contributions in helping others. And I have a pleasurable lifestyle. I would not have gotten here had I not taken my PROVE IT journey. And though I'm living on this mountaintop, I understand it is not a destination. I am not in anyone's box; I can change my *mind* and choose again.

There is a beginning, a middle, and an end to everything. The success of the company Brad and I built served its purpose. It fulfilled my initial definition of success. We built a great life for ourselves and our sons. Once its purpose was served, moving on was a choice I had to make. I could have pleased the people around me (giving in to outside pressure) by hitting a new gear of contorting to meet expectations, but I would have missed everything that was waiting for me on the other side of that door.

On the mountaintop, I live from within, honor my intuition, express my creativity, and fully use my physical senses to experience life.

My grandmother once made the point that people in the Bible pitched tents—they were always ready to move to their next destination. The day Brad left my office and I sat stunned by his decision, I didn't recognize the call to pack my tent. I didn't have a mountaintop mindset. I could have celebrated Brad's departure and begun the process of planning my own.

It took courage to carry the business through tumultuous times for three and a half years. But it took more courage to walk away from it and start at the bottom of a new mountain. Sometimes all we need is the courage to take that one step forward—the step of mindset shifting. I didn't have a sheet of answers to work from, but each time I focused my attention on my mindset I found a better pathway forward.

I stay mindful about a few simple facts. Like, money is nothing more than energy. Its only tangible value is how it is used. When we use money to care for family, friends, and community, we circulate an energy of love. When we use money to hoard and overindulge in personal possessions, we circulate the energy of selfishness. When we spend our money to unify and promote positive ideas and actions for the good of humanity, we circulate the energy of care and collaboration. On the other hand, when we use money to self-promote and exalt divisive ideologies, we circulate the energy of separatism. Money used to promote safe spaces for individual differences circulates an energy of inclusivity. And money that is used to promote judgment and stoke fear is an energy that can lead to harmful prejudices, oppression, civil violence, and war.

Like money, people are energy in our lives as well. They represent values and influences that help shape who we are. This can be great when the energies are positive, uplifting, and in sync with our goals. But if we are not conscious, we can unintentionally integrate energies that create complexities and discord. Worse yet, the impact of those energies can disrupt our lives long after the people who created them have moved on. This happens in relationships, jobs, and friendships, and even with beliefs. But we can recognize these energies before we let them in. Our bodies typically communicate sensations (tension, irritability, anxiety, etc.); we just have to pay attention.

However, I learned to examine my own energy before deciding the problem is outside me. Is it possible that there is something in me that invited the energy dynamic in? Did I want something I thought it could give me? Was there something about it I envied and wanted to be close to? Had I contorted in the first place to have it? There is always a role I play in creating relationship energies. So my first task, before blaming or removing any energy out of my life, is to look to any part I might be playing in keeping it alive. Sometimes that's all that is needed.

I work daily to live consciously with a PROVE IT awareness. I don't always feel courageous in doing it but it is said that once you know something you can't unknow it. Climbing my new mountain required me to slow way down so I could move from relying on external rules and logic to trusting inner feelings and that soft, calm voice inside. I practiced honoring caution, not fear. Caution is the voice of reason that guides me as I move toward what I want; it doesn't talk me out of what I desire. Fear, on the other hand, is loud and uncompromising. It's the voice that clouds my head with everything that not only could but also "will" go wrong. Fear hates risk, and fear will tell you whatever is necessary to get you to avoid it. The voice of fear should be reserved for real danger—which for most of us is rare. Caution helps me avoid harm. Fear makes me avoid life. Caution is what is needed for any new climb.

It took a few years for Brad and me to completely release our old identities and discover a way to explain our transition and transformation to other people in fifteen seconds or less. But no matter how much we tried to say it plainly and simply that we decided to wipe the slate clean and start over, it seemed people were uncomfortable accepting our truth. Change can be hard even for the ones not directly going through it. After deconstructing our company (within three years of Brad returning, we let all the contracts end), we sat in our two-person office, looking at each other. It was uncomfortable, but as I said, sometimes the answer is to sit still.

We started to get calls—random calls from companies and people. They wanted advice, coaching, training, and strategic planning. We didn't plan the path; it naturally presented itself. In fact, we did absolutely no marketing for any of the clients we have supported since we pivoted. We stood at the bottom of a new mountain, unsure of everything except what we both felt inside: a desire to rediscover, realign, and redirect toward a new purpose. Living in purpose on purpose gives more than happiness; it gives joy.

Our old mountain was in the rearview mirror. It had given us its best view. As I type these words, hoping my PROVE IT journey helps anyone who reads about it, I am grateful for every challenge that knocked me down and even more grateful I had the courage to evaluate my mindset and then choose differently each time I got back up.

Brad and I continue to evolve. We learned to not imprison ourselves with expectations and boxes to fit in. On our new mountain, Brad and I have shared and separate paths now. Together, Brad and I authored this book; it is part of the new mountain we share. But still, we keep our backpacks ready, untethered to its current beautiful view and remain open to our next climb.

Seven Mountain Climb Lessons

Mountain climbing is an opportunity to master terrain and ascend to new elevations. Climbing requires having an open mind and engaging in mindshifts along the way. Each challenge on the climb presents the climber with the choice to focus and exert energy on fighting to stay firm on the ground where they stand or on the opportunity to take steps to ascend from where they are. I've learned to have joy on the climb and to honor my challenges along the way as a potential lift to a new level. As I climb, I keep the following lessons with me.

1. *It isn't just about how high you can go (the ascent).* Enjoy the sights, experiences, and discoveries along the way.
2. *Climbing is easier with a lighter load.* Carrying too much stuff requires more stops and causes fatigue. Unload what isn't necessary for a more exhilarating experience.
3. *Be prepared for unexpected forces of nature; they will happen.* The timing of external events is not predictable, so be sure to have the right tools in place (mindset, mindshift, mindful practices) so you can adapt quickly.
4. *Maintain a routine for healthy nourishment.* The journey can be physically and emotionally strenuous. Consume healthy foods and do things that increase and keep your energy high.
5. *Breaks are necessary.* Reenergize between climbs. It is important to get acclimated and adjust as you reach higher altitudes.
6. *Maintain strength of mind.* Psychological strength is imperative for optimism and endurance. Practice deep breathing, avoid

looking too often at the giant slopes ahead, and keep an eye on maintaining secure footing on the current ground holding you.

7. *Take in the view and admire the magnificence.* Don't let the effort of the climb steal from the beauty of the mountain. Soak in its gifts, and remember that the climb is only one step at a time.

There are things I miss about my old mountain, and I keep those positive memories with me. As for the things I don't miss, I keep those too—not as memories but as valuable lessons. My current mountain has given me hills to climb, but most of them continue to strengthen and enlighten me. But the biggest and most significant lesson for me is the understanding that my plans are just a suggestion to the universe because together, we are co-creators of my experiences.

I chased success, but success does not have to be chased. When I focused on being happy, I attracted it.

When the view where you are no longer inspires you, when you feel like you're losing your footing and have fears about the future, when you find yourself resisting truths about your circumstances, when life feels like a constant struggle bringing you much more stress than pleasure—evaluate and shift your strategy. Maybe you aren't climbing your mountain with the right mindset (level of consciousness). Or maybe you're not climbing your own mountain.

How do you know if it is your mountain? When that mountain calls you and you can't resist the beauty of what it offers. When you consider taking a leap of faith just for the chance to know it. When you find you must talk yourself out of loving it but still think about it. When, finally, you are willing to release the old one to find out.

• • •

The PROVE IT journey was a double-sided experience. As I pushed through my revelations, so did Brad. Brad tells me he was disillusioned by his ego during the peak of my crisis, and he cannot recall his exact state of mind as life was happening. He says the days we spent arguing are a blur to him.

In the next several chapters, Brad walks you through his journey back to himself. His story starts with a realization of all the collateral damage that unfolded during a time he describes as unconscious ego domination.

PROVE IT LESSON

Don't cheat yourself out of the full experience of life by making yourself small enough to match what the world is telling you it can handle. We should compromise but not contort. We are individual creations of beauty, never intended to be like anyone else. If you feel something inside calling you, don't kill it before giving it a chance to emerge. Listen to the voice of caution, not fear.

PROVE IT QUESTIONS

- How do I like the view from the mountain I'm on?
- Is there something I talk myself out of, something I'm telling myself I can't be or do?
- Am I building success (feeling good about my work, commitments, and contributions, and creating a pleasurable lifestyle)?

PROVE IT MINDFUL PRACTICES

Imagine rewriting your script, even if you are currently successful. Release prior experiences, block out preconceived obstacles, and write a vision that makes you excited. As you write, focus first on a state of "being" and not doing. For example, being happy, peaceful, carefree, wealthy, inspired, content, or all of the above. Then think about and write all the things you do, can do, or have done that create the opportunity for you to be those things. Next, list the choices you have to create and expand what is on your list so you can create more of what you choose to be. Remember, listen to the voice of caution, not fear, and start climbing.

For the comprehensive PROVE IT Mindshifts Journaling Guide, please refer to the appendix.

PART II

BRAD

I BELIEVE THAT EVERY HUMAN being at some point in their life wants to live the most successful and fulfilled life they possibly can. There is no shortage of opinions on how to do this, and considering that people all have different strengths, weaknesses, talents, and skills, there is certainly no one-size-fits-all answer. Given this, it makes sense to go with the "people have to do what works for them" approach. But there are several factors that can affect what works and what doesn't. Life experiences, resources, environment, emotional stability, age, race, ethnicity, geographic location, and so on can have an impact.

Now that I am in my middle age, I have experienced a lot, and I have observed the experiences of others as well. My experiences include the death of my parents while I was in college, a thirty-seven-year marriage, being a father to two sons, operating a business side by side with my wife for more than thirty years, growing that business into a multimillion-dollar company regarded as an industry leader, being significantly affected by sudden and unpredictable business industry changes, and figuring out how to weather that storm.

Through all my experiences, I can say without a doubt that the most significant factor that has influenced both my successes and my failures is me. Nothing else comes close. In a lot of ways, this is good news, since I have total control over myself and what I do, which places me in control of my own destiny. Great! But wait—not so fast. What if I don't work hard enough or I make bad decisions or I don't have the talent or skills to be great at what I am doing? Well, that would probably mean that I wouldn't be very successful, wouldn't it?

Not necessarily. Fortunately, that was not the case for me when my wife, Malitta, and I started our business in the early 1990s. I worked hard and managed to make mostly good decisions. I didn't have every talent and skill needed for success, but what I didn't have Malitta had, and what we didn't have, we figured out how to get. We covered all the bases. This is why, at one point, our company was referred to as the "gold standard" of federal conference and event management by one of the most respected gurus of our industry.

However, change is certain, and it can happen almost instantaneously. In business, yes, but what I'm referring to is the change that happened in me. In the book *Ego Is the Enemy* by Ryan Holiday, I read that we should be humble in our aspirations, gracious in our successes, and resilient in our failures.[1] My mindset and behavior during some of the most successful years of our business did not reflect this sage advice. And because of that, my results changed for the worse. There had been a stage in my career when I was totally in the zone, churning out one success after another. Then I hit a period when I just could not find that zone, and this caused me to lose confidence and develop self-doubt, something that anyone who knew me, including me, would never have imagined.

My story outlines the mindset shift that had to happen for me to find my zone again. After I returned to the company, I had to PROVE IT to myself that I was ready to shift to a new mindset and stay there. My hope is that by sharing my story of personal transformation, I provide a blueprint for success to people who are trying to find that zone where they have joy and live their best life.

I must emphasize though that the experiences I share changed me in ways that were necessary for my long-term growth and transformation as a person, husband, father, and leader. *But* the crisis I created to achieve that personal transformation was not the only pathway to get there. There was a better way. I could have had a more open mindset and less selfish behaviors that would have allowed me to listen more, see my blind spots, and change voluntarily rather than being forced into it by the circumstances I created.

Malitta's story largely focuses on what she experienced, managed, and learned during the period of turmoil after I left our company and the ensuing storm that rocked our worlds. My story starts at the same point as Malitta's in 2010, when I left our company, but largely focuses on my experience after returning to the company in the aftermath of the storm that Malitta managed and what I experienced, suffered, and learned from it.

So, please, come along with me on my journey to mindset freedom.

CHAPTER 8

PAIN TO PRESENCE

> Pain is the breaking of the shell that
> encloses your understanding.
> —**KAHLIL GIBRAN, "ON PAIN"**

THE KEY TO FORWARD MOVEMENT in life is to act and to act in our conscious mind. Failure to act leaves us at our starting point, and if that place is one that is painful or puts us at risk, it is not a place where we want to stay. There are several circumstances that can make us not act, but in the end, our paralysis is most often caused by fear. Fear of failure, fear of experiencing physical or emotional pain, fear of losing control, fear of losing money, fear of embarrassment, fear of losing security, fear of being exposed—fear, fear, fear. We all have something we are afraid of—whether we face it and admit it or not. Fear is the real f-word. It is the action stopper. It is what my spiritual mentor calls stinkin' thinkin'.

Once we give into fear, helplessness can set in, and depending on how deep the fear is, this can lead to forms of depression. For me, this state of immobility became what I call my pain body. When I live in my pain body, I seem to bring other things to me that just make everything worse. In my pain body, I don't sleep, I drink more than I would like, I give off negative energy to people around me, and instead of spending my time in the present moment where action exists, I live in past regrets or future worries. At this point, it feels as though my feet are locked in dried concrete.

This is typically when I am having full-blown conversations with myself. I tell myself, *Brad, you have got to get out of your pain body and into your power body, or you are going to allow the things you are afraid of happening to happen.*

A close cousin to fear is ego. I refer to ego as a cousin to fear rather than a sibling because it blocks your pathway to joy and success in a different way. Fear causes inaction while ego causes wrong action. By wrong action, I mean thoughts, decisions, and behaviors that are driven by inflated or deflated self-esteem. In both cases, we can end up with outside-in thinking—thinking that is based more on what things look like to others than on what they really are.

Ego is our sense of who we are; it drives self-esteem. Ego doesn't have to be a bad thing; it can be a source of confidence for us that allows us to believe in ourselves and perform at high levels. But when our sense of self comes from the wrong place—outside us—we become dependent on what other people think about us to feel good about ourselves. This is where our ego can become a liability rather than an asset. It isn't hard to imagine the trouble we can get ourselves into when our source of ego or self comes from what other people think or tell us about us. The ego has two siblings: being egocentric—thinking everything is about us—and being egotistical—having an inflated view of our self-importance. I refer to ego throughout this book because understanding it was my biggest lesson during my journey.

You may be all too familiar with fear and its ride-or-die partner ego. But are you self-aware about how they affect your life? If so, you will be comforted to read about how they affected me. If not, my story may open your eyes to a potential blind spot.

As you've read, in 2010 I made one decision that put in motion a chain of events that drew pain into my life in a huge way. I left the company that Malitta and I built and successfully ran for two decades to take a politically appointed job in local government. At the time, our company had achieved record sales and profits, but we were facing a transition, some of which we were planning for and some we had no idea were coming.

As you've read in Malitta's story, we had planned on the need to replace revenue because we were becoming ineligible for some of the federal contract work in our market, and we were in the middle of developing strategies to sustain the business. This was challenging, but we had done it successfully before—we faced similar transitions five years and ten years prior but managed to double and then triple our revenue.

However, the 2010 challenge was more significant, and my ego was much bigger. *Ego Is the Enemy* says that when our ego becomes too large, confidence becomes arrogance, assertiveness becomes obstinance, and self-assurance becomes reckless abandon.[1] I had become obstinate and began to make reckless decisions. My decision to leave the company was reckless and selfish. Everybody makes bad decisions at some point, sure, but I was about to string together a few mindless decisions that will make your head spin.

Malitta was clear with me; she tried to convince me that it was a terrible idea. She was extremely uncomfortable with my decision to leave the company. When she pushed back, my obstinance kicked in, and I convinced myself that it was a good time for me to leave. I told myself that the company needed new and better leadership—that I was not effectively moving us forward, so it was a good time for Malitta to take over. To make things worse, I acted like an immature ass and used how much Malitta loved me and wanted me to be happy to shame her into giving in.

I was ignoring one *big* thing. We had built this company *together*.

Together, she and I were the secret leadership sauce that gave our company its world-class flavor—executing projects on six continents across the globe. Let me be clear here: When I made my decision, I was not consciously aware of what I was doing. My unconscious mind was driving my thinking, allowing my ego to take over and cloud my judgment.

My enlightened thoughts on fear, ego, error thinking, and unconscious mind can all be rolled up into one word: *mindset*. Mindset is our attitude or beliefs that drive behavior in a particular area. In her book *Mindset*, Carol Dweck teaches that, in general, mindsets come in two broad buckets: fixed and growth. Fixed mindsets are a barrier to growth because they don't support change. They often result from us not listening to and embracing feedback from those around us, resulting in decisions made in isolation and with incomplete information (which tend to be bad). Growth mindsets support improvement through listening and change.[2] I eventually learned that my mindset needed to shift from fixed to growth. The PROVE IT methodology is the tool I used on my mindshift journey.

So why would anyone in their right mind operate with a fixed mindset? They don't see what they are doing because they aren't embracing feedback and other points of view. They are often suffering from ego or fear-based thinking, which blocks their pathway to a growth mindset. What does this look like? Maybe your ego is telling you that you are smarter than the people trying to get through to you or your fear is telling you that a perspective different than yours is going to harm you. The bottom line is that we may need a change in mindset—a mindshift—to grow. But unfortunately, we can block our own ability to have a mindshift by allowing error thinking to close our minds, which means we remain stuck in a fixed mindset.

There was another major factor that caused me to leave the company, a collision of my ego and my fears. As I mentioned, the company's transition meant developing new business—and that required hiring new business development people. We had never had much success with hiring business development people, so I took on much of this responsibility myself.

Business development people can be farmers or hunters. Farmers develop business from the clients and customers the company already has. Hunters go out and find new customers, capture them, and bring back new business opportunities. These are very different skill sets.

Our transition required hunting skills. I'd had some success in prior years hunting for new business when the company expanded our conference and meeting planning services from the federal government to the pharmaceutical industry. But as I was doing that, Malitta was questioning some of the decisions I was making about new personnel. This created some mild tension between us, but the tension remained mild because we were having success getting new clients. But the new situation we faced required more intense hunting. Growth within the pharma industry was slow—too slow to replace the federal contract work we were going to lose. So not only did we have to hunt for new contracts; we had to win contracts outside our established wheelhouse in information technology. I was not so successful with this type of hunting.

I felt like people in the company saw me struggling, especially Malitta. I wasn't creating success fast enough. Malitta told me that some of the employees I had assembled to help me with the hunt were not the best choices and that I was not effectively managing them. The poor results combined with Malitta's feedback bruised my ego, and I became defensive. Rather than having a growth mindset and changing course based on her feedback, I stuck with my fixed mindset, ignored her suggestions, and continued with what wasn't working.

The lackluster results kicked up my fear of failure, and when fear started steering the ship, it collided with my ego. At the time, I was unconscious of what was going on, but that collision drained my confidence and made me even more fearful. I started looking for a lifeboat to save my sinking self-esteem. The offer of a new, high-profile, politically appointed job was just that, boosting my ego and self-esteem.

So I left the company. My ego issues only got worse after I left. I performed at a high level in my new job, achieving goals that were praised by my boss, the public, and the media. (Yes, I read my own press and believed it.) This sounds arrogant, doesn't it? I had never considered myself to be arrogant; I have never looked at other people like I am better than them, no matter who they are. My parents taught me that a person's job (or lack of job) or status in life was no basis for how they deserved to be treated. We all deserve to be treated with respect. I thought this was enough to make me humble.

But I missed something.

Malitta tried to point out (I would learn to listen to her later) that, although I did not look down on people, I did have a sense that I could do things that other people could not. Of course, at the time, my fixed mindset was not embracing her feedback, and I did not consider her perspective. I thought my relentless pursuit of knowledge through reading and learning made me more equipped to do certain things better than other people. I thought I was proving this by generating win after win in my new job. One day, someone told me that everything I touched turned to gold—silently, I agreed. In contrast to Malitta's input, this feedback supported my error thinking, so I more than embraced it.

Between outside media and on-the-job flattery, my ego grew, and it felt good. My ego gave me a sense of security that I had lost when both my parents died while I was in college. Of course, I didn't realize it at the time. I made this connection years later after facing the fallout of my decision to leave the company and taking a hard look at myself. As it was happening, my growing ego made me even more obstinate, and I was deaf to my wife's alarms that the transition the company needed to make was much bigger than what we had anticipated. She warned me after I left that if we didn't act—if I didn't return to and reconnect with the business—the company would shrink in a way we had never seen. I hadn't given her or the company time for my transition. When I left, she had no replacement for what I brought to the business. The water had gotten rough, and I had left her alone to steer the ship.

For nearly three years, I ignored Malitta's cries for me to return to the company and bring back the missing ingredient to our success. I resisted, and this, combined with other business circumstances, led to a decline in revenue and employee layoffs—something we had never experienced before. This whirlwind of challenges rocked Malitta's world, and our relationship. I avoided the problems by further immersing myself in my government job and my accomplishments. The company's plight eventually slapped me toward the reality I had been ignoring, and I began to see the impact of our personal and business challenges. I could no longer ignore what Malitta was trying to tell me. The challenges we faced required both of us to fully engage.

My ego was about to take a big tumble. I returned to the company in 2014. I realized how much my string of ego-based decisions had damaged Malitta's trust in me, and this hurt me badly. My decision to leave had left Malitta in a mess and damaged the company we had spent the majority of our married life building. I feared the future. I also started to see what I had done to her and how selfish and stupid my behavior had been. This threw me into full pain body mode, but I still did not understand at this point that the root cause of my issue was ego. Instead, I locked in on the impact of my poor decision, and because I was so consumed by the mistake, I was unable to be present enough to do anything about it. I could not move forward.

It was clear that the wins in my government job were just losses for the company and, most importantly, my family. The challenge of replacing and rebuilding now (versus when I left) required a lot more. I blamed myself, did not forgive myself, and called myself an idiot every day—among other confidence-degrading thoughts.

I lived in my pain body until a Sunday I will never forget. I went to a church in Washington, DC, the church Malitta had been attending for a couple of years. I had gone to the church a few times with her before. On this Sunday morning, I sat in a pew at the church and heard the minister say, "You are either living in a beautiful state of harmony or a state of suffering."

I looked up from my sleepy nodding and said to myself, *That's me!* This simple statement grabbed me and started me down a path of self-introspection that would last a few years. It was the start of a mindshift.

I call this mindshift the journey within, or my excavation. I began to realize that I had to save myself by moving away from the regrets of the past and fears of the future to a focus on the opportunities of the present. I had to stop turning in circles and take action. I had to focus my energy on new choices. I needed to shift my mindset and return to the kind of purpose-driven thinking that allowed Malitta and me to grow a successful and values-driven company in the first place. I was beginning the journey to reconnecting to my purpose.

All of this is nicely summed up in this quote from the book *The Seven Spiritual Laws of Success* by Deepak Chopra:

> Therefore, success in life depends on knowing who we really are. When our internal reference point is our spirit, our true self, we experience all the power of our spirit. When our internal reference point is the ego or self-image, we feel cut off from our source and the uncertainty of events creates fear and doubt. The ego is influenced by objects outside the Self—circumstances, people, and things. It thrives on the approval of others. It wants to control because it lives in fear. But the ego is not really who we are. The ego is our social mask, it is the role we are playing.[3]

From all of this, I have come to believe that anyone can learn from their own experiences, but a big component of wisdom is learning from the feedback and experiences of others. If we can do this, we can be enlightened before we have crisis situations. I didn't choose the path that would have avoided a crisis. If you haven't had the pre-enlightenment crisis, try to avoid it—it's much easier. When I look back, it's clear. I could have avoided my crisis. If I had listened to and embraced Malitta's concerns, things would have been very different. But my ego had control of me, and it produced error thinking. It told me that what I wanted was most important. That lie created a whole bunch of other lies in my mind to support it. All that error thinking resulted in a fixed mindset and mindless decisions.

Anyone can learn from their own experiences, but a big component of wisdom is learning from the feedback and experiences of others.

PROVE IT LESSON

Presence put me on the pathway to finding my purpose. Once I was on this pathway, a growth mindset pointed me toward my purpose. I had to be in the present, not the past or the future, to have the awareness to keep a growth mindset and chase away a fixed mindset. This lesson is the source of a personal quote that I always try to remember: "Enlightenment often follows a crisis, but it doesn't have to; it's my choice."

PROVE IT QUESTIONS

- Do I have a fixed mindset about a particular experience or life area that is a barrier to moving from a place of pain to the present (for example, sticking to a position about something and refusing to consider another point of view)?
- What causes my mindset to be fixed? Fear? Ego?
- Do I need to figure out what is keeping me in a fixed mindset so I can live in the present and develop a growth mindset?

PROVE IT MINDFUL PRACTICES

- *Opposition thinking.* When your mind is generating thoughts of pain, invoke the opposite thought: being grateful that you are past the experience that generated the pain. It may still be painful, but we are past the experience. Express gratitude for that.

- *Journaling.* Daily journaling helps us to be present. I ran across this simple format. It has had a profound impact on changing my behaviors to more of what I want and less of what I don't. It's called My Morning BAGELS (without the carbs):
  - Behaviors for me to focus on today
  - Affirmations for positive energy and attitude today
  - Goals to keep in front of me today (and beyond)
  - Evaluation of what happened yesterday
  - Lessons I learned yesterday and need to remember
  - Successes I achieved yesterday

- *Move from mind full to mindful.* Find a regular activity to do when your mind is so filled with thoughts about the past and future or all the things you have to get done. Examples are:
  - Getting outside in the light
  - Moving! Walk, run, or engage in whatever form of movement works for you
  - Listening to music or reading
  - Any activity that allows you to slow your thoughts and clear your mind

CHAPTER 9

RESISTANCE TO RELEASE

> We all have blind spots in our knowledge and opinions. The bad news is that they can leave us blind to our blindness, which gives us false confidence in our judgment and prevents us from rethinking.
> —ADAM GRANT, *THINK AGAIN: THE POWER OF KNOWING WHAT YOU DON'T KNOW*

MY EGOTISTICAL AND EGOCENTRIC THINKING and behavior landed me in a life predicament that put me on a path of self-awareness. The process of getting out of my pain body required me to take the journey. When I began moving out of my pain body, I had not reconnected with my purpose. It was an interesting place to be because not being self-aware is like being unable to see in a dark room and trying to find your way out.

This reminds me of the concept from Tasha Eurich's book, *Insight*, that self-awareness is the foundation for growth, but without recognizing our blind spots, we'll be stuck repeating the same patterns over and over.[1] How can we be expected to fix what we can't see? Guess what? *We can't!*

So how did I tackle my blind spot challenge? First, I accepted the fact that I was in a state of suffering because of my behavior. Then I faced truths about myself by listening to someone who observed my behavior. I call this process looking in the mirror. This is harder for some of us than others. For me, it was difficult because looking in the mirror brought back pain. But half the battle was deciding to find that mirror and look into it so I could see myself clearly. Who was I and who had I become? These are the questions that bounced off the mirror once I decided to find the truth and face it.

The best mirrors are the people who know us well enough to give us honest feedback about our behavior or personality traits. Finding a mirror is not always easy. When we aren't careful, we discourage or repel people who could be that mirror for us. We do this both consciously (intentionally) and unconsciously (unknowingly). We tend to have thorns or sore spots—sensitivities—that we protect, and we don't let people near them in an attempt to avoid pain or getting to the truth about ourselves. This allows blind spots—and the pain that comes with them—to not only persist but grow. How do we discourage and repel? We use emotional reactions to attack or deflect the mirror to keep them from exposing the thorn or sore spot we'd rather not face. Emotional reactions can come in different forms, depending on who you are: contempt, criticism, defensiveness, and stonewalling are the ones John Gottman describes as the Four Horsemen of the Apocalypse. His writing on these behaviors helped me understand how I used these four emotional reactions to defend the sore spots that shielded me from my blind spots.[2] The Four Horsemen are:

Contempt. This may be the worst of the horsemen. This is when we are condescending to the other person and show no respect for them. It often comes in the form of name-calling, threats, or insults. We put the other person down, expressing our superiority (maybe even mocking them), and declare war!

Criticism. This is blaming the other person by expressing that there is something wrong with them or who they are. It's when we attack another person's character or flaws. Pointing out the way someone is *behaving* can be effective, but criticizing who they *are* as a person can be damaging and is rarely productive.

Defensiveness. (My horseman of choice.) This is when we feel personally attacked and take position to protect ourselves. The "attack" can be as simple as someone telling us to remember to take out the trash. The defense we give back can ward off the perceived attack and effectively keep something true about us or our behavior hidden from sight (like, perhaps the real problem is we resent being told when and what to do). The goal is to make the other person stand down.

Stonewalling. This is when we disengage because we are "flooded" by the feedback we receive from someone else. The disengagement sends the message that either we are not listening or we are ignoring the feedback. This can incite the other person and actually intensify their attack.

For example, when Malitta pointed out to me in 2010 that I was making an ego-based decision to leave the company, she tried to tell me I was only thinking about what was best for me. That was my egocentric sore spot, and I needed her to leave it alone because facing it would have possibly changed my mindset and my decision. I didn't want that because I wanted what I wanted. See all those *I*'s in the previous sentence? Another sign that egocentricity is in the house! My thoughts were fixated on me. I jumped up on my favorite of the Four Horsemen, defensiveness. I made myself out to be a victim and made Malitta feel bad about victimizing me and not letting me do what I wanted, and it worked. Malitta eventually accepted that I was going to leave the company.

I know what you may be thinking: Did I do this consciously or unconsciously? Clearly it was unconscious because I didn't understand how the conscious and unconscious minds work at that point in my life. It was the unconscious nature of my behavior that actually made my sore spot a blind spot. (I explain the unconscious mind and behavior shortly.) Again, the tactic of using emotional reactions is how we teach people to manage around our thorns and sore spots, which allows us to protect the sensitive areas we don't want to face. When a person tries to point us toward a truth about ourselves and we attack or repel them, they often lose their will to keep going down that road. They tell themselves that it isn't worth it because pressing the issue could break us or ruin our relationship. So they don't touch our sore spots, and we (the blind) end up losing. The mirrors that can show us our blind spots crack and shatter from our defense tactics. And what do we do? We go on about our business with the blind spot, fixed mindset, and thorns (sore spots) all intact. That is until a crisis happens—a crisis gets our attention, softens our hard head, and makes us more receptive to feedback. After my own lesson, I now notice how often people "train" those closest to them to not touch their sore spots.

Remember, enlightenment typically follows crisis, but it doesn't have to; it's our choice. Instead, we can choose to honor the mirrors in our life on our own when we receive hints that self-introspection is needed, such as hearing similar feedback about our behavior from multiple people or someone who knows us well. Or we can wait to get smacked by life. Malitta described this awakening as getting hit by a two-by-four, a challenge or crisis that comes from our choice to not take right action to avoid it. The two-by-four creates "no choice but to deal with it now" situations.

Ideally, we pick up the mirror on our own to voluntarily search for blind spots before a crisis, but we don't often choose this route. Voluntarily looking in the mirror is more or less challenging depending on how "blind" we are and how resistant we are to surrendering ego, fear, or whatever has a grip on our mind and how we are thinking. Of course, I waited to get hit by the two-by-four, and after getting hit, I was shaken enough to look in my mirror. I started to see things I should have seen long ago, before it arrived.

I was in a pitch-black room until I saw a flicker of light—the minister's "beautiful state of harmony" lesson. My feeling of enlightenment when I heard those words was palpable. I sat in the church, pulled out my cell phone, and started typing what has now become a library of notes that is 11,000 words and counting. That is where I wanted to be—in that "beautiful" place and not "the state of suffering," which was the darkness I had been living in. I needed a mirror. Where was it? Was it on my bathroom wall or in the bedroom? Neither. Again, those mirrors don't talk back to us, and if they do, they aren't effective because, as Muhammed Ali said, "Your hands can't hit what your eyes can't see." My blind spots were my sources of suffering that I couldn't see yet.

Ideally, we pick up the mirror on our own to voluntarily search for blind spots before a crisis, but we don't often choose this route.

As it turns out, I had a few mirrors. As I stated earlier, the best mirror for me was Malitta. My experience is that the best mirror is the person who knows you better than anyone else. It doesn't have to be a spouse or partner, but it must be someone you trust, who knows you well. Someone who is so confident in what they see and cares so much about your well-being that they won't let your emotional reactions (the horsemen) scare them off. A mirror must be able to stand up to our reactions. To help us, they have to stick to their guns until we get out of our feelings, get quiet, listen, and go within. This could take days, weeks, or months, but the mirror must stand strong. Malitta is a rock, and she stood strong. It took me four to six months after understanding that I needed a mirror to accept the reflections of my blind spots I was getting back. Once I did, I reached for more help: books, sermon lessons, and discussions with my sons.

How did this acceptance of my blind spots change me? I believe the most important change in my behavior was learning the power of pause. Pausing allowed me to be more present, conscious, and aware. I learned to truly listen to what Malitta was telling me to understand and empathize with what she was saying—rather than listening to figure out how I was going to respond and refute what she was saying. This awareness of the power of pause actually took me back to ten years before, when a psychologist suggested I might have had a serotonin imbalance that actually reduced my power to pause.

Serotonin is a neurotransmitter that helps with regulating mood. It is made by the body's nerve cells and works throughout the body but mainly in the intestines, brain, and blood. Our bodies can produce too much or too little of it. Low levels of it are thought to contribute to depression. I was told my serotonin levels were low. I even took medication on and off for a while to help raise my serotonin levels so I could listen more and react less. But at that time, while I understood intellectually what the psychologist was telling me about serotonin, my lack of self-awareness did not allow me to see the impact on my behavior. So I didn't take the medication regularly.

It wasn't until my two-by-four experience, followed by the "state of suffering" words I heard in church pointing me to the journey within, that self-awareness allowed me to see how I was using defensiveness. This is when I began pausing long enough for what Malitta was telling me to sink into my mind and consciousness in a way that shifted my mindset. My discussions with her started ending more often with me walking away quiet and reflective rather than debating why my point of view was right or me trying to flip the conversation back to what she was doing wrong. That trick of flipping the script on your mirror to make them doubt what they are telling you is a classic tool used by those of us who allow defensiveness to hide our blind spots. Some refer to this as gaslighting. I was well-versed in the use of this tool, but as I paused more and used my conscious mind to manage my behavior, I controlled the habit of picking up the torch and stopped the gaslighting. This was practicing the power of pause.

Instead of the serotonin medication, over the years I have developed the use of another form of MEDS: meditation, exercise, diet, and sleep (I cover this more later). I strongly believe my use of MEDS increased my serotonin levels and helped me pause and listen, and this is supported by research.[3]

Accepting feedback allowed me to peel back some layers of blockage and figure out who I was before experiences in life got ahold of me. I started to rediscover my truer self—that person put here with all the talents and gifts needed to carry out my purpose, like all of us are before the world gets ahold of us and we develop bad habits. My ego challenges were in plain sight. Don't get me wrong, ego was not the only thing reflected in my mirrors, but it was at the root cause of my state of suffering.

The good news is that, along the journey, I found some good things in my mirrors, too. Having conversations about myself opened me to remembering my true self—it was hidden but still there. I rediscovered my love of learning and sharing knowledge. I remembered that as a kid, I had taught myself to fish from a book, and as a teenager I voraciously studied World War II and the assassination of President John F. Kennedy. Looking in the mirror, I reconnected with my love for studying and sharing knowledge with other people. I saw someone who feels passion when he can help others navigate and succeed. Someone who loved the experience of coaching kids in basketball. I saw a seasoned, compassionate coach and leader.

When I stopped resisting the parts of my reflection my Malitta mirror was showing me and began to trust her reflection, I was able to dig deeper and find some of the good stuff I needed. Mirrors aren't just for the bad stuff; they can give us inspiring truths as well. I was moving further into my journey toward purpose and away from pain.

I understand that much of what manifested from the blockages and blemishes in my life resided in my unconscious mind. Self-awareness was the first step to shifting away from being unconscious and becoming more conscious. I had no idea I had an ego issue until it was pointed out to me. With this awareness, I was able to attack my issue by seeking out and understanding its source. The work of redirecting my ego source from outside me to inside was part of my journey within.

My conscious attack on ego has neutralized and reduced it to a healthy level, one where I am confident but not egocentric or egotistical. A level where I have self-esteem, but not self-importance. My ego is not dead but rather alive at a level that is an asset and not a liability. Be clear about this though: I still get egotistical or egocentric thoughts. But I have pulled them into my conscious mind where I am aware of them and away from unconscious, autopilot behaviors.

When you move from resistance to release, you let go and flow with life (with a mind like water) and stop fighting to steer the ship where your fixed mindset wants it to go.

PROVE IT LESSON

Blind spots are a barrier to self-awareness. Self-awareness is the foundation of real personal transformation because if you can't see and accept what needs to change in you, you can't change it.

PROVE IT QUESTIONS

- Who is the mirror that helps me to be self-aware?
- Do I listen to the feedback the mirror gives me, or do I use the Four Horsemen to shut them down?

- Do I pause, get quiet, listen, and contemplate the feedback my mirror is giving me?

PROVE IT MINDFUL PRACTICES

- Find a true mirror, someone who you trust and who knows you well. Give them permission to tell you the truth.

- When that mirror starts reflecting to you what they see, don't attack them. Pause first, and then listen. That is the pathway to seeing your blind spots and becoming self-aware.

- After pausing, listening, and reflecting, practice accepting who you are by going on the journey within. On the journey, use the power of your presence to see behaviors and habits as they are happening. Decide which of these behaviors and habits should be kept and those that need to be released. Presence + Self-Awareness = Release and Transformation.

CHAPTER 10

OBSTACLES TO OBSERVATION

The observer changes reality by the very act of observation.
—DEEPAK CHOPRA, *THE BOOK OF SECRETS*

ONE OF THE MOST POWERFUL mindshifts I have learned to make is to operate not as a participant but instead as an observer of what I am living through in any given moment. When life is happening and we are riding the ups and downs, it can feel like we're riding a roller coaster, queasy and scared. But imagine if we could watch ourselves experience life rather than just live it. We'd watch ourselves on the roller coaster, thinking, *Brad, you look crazy with all the yelling and screaming you are doing—just get quiet and take the ride.*

By using our powers of observation, we can better see who we are being as we are living through the experiences. If we can see ourselves, we can consciously choose the way we think and behave in the moment and objectively look back at past behavior as lessons that can help us. Likewise, when we encounter obstacles to happiness, contentment, and success, becoming an observer rather than a participant can allow us to see opportunities we might not be able to otherwise see. It's like having a hurdle in front of us when we are participating at ground level, but when we rise up to be an observer, we can see the way around the hurdle. In this chapter, I share what I learned as I shifted from experiencing obstacles to observing opportunities.

As I share my obstacles to observation experience, it would be helpful for me to share some information about the three levels of the mind. Malitta and I refer to them at different points throughout our stories. There are numerous research studies dating back to the 1890s about the levels of mind.[1] While the research does not reflect a clear consensus, there is general agreement about the existence of the conscious and unconscious minds and that they do affect our behavior. In current-day use, we most often see references to the conscious, subconscious, and unconscious minds. In some cases, the terms *subconscious mind* and *unconscious mind* are used interchangeably. Sigmund Freud's research on the three levels of the mind continues to exert a significant influence on how people think about the mind.[2] In this book, we use Freud's explanations of the conscious, subconscious (sometimes called preconscious), and unconscious minds as our reference point. Here's what these terms mean in our words:

- *Conscious mind.* The thoughts, memories, and feelings we are aware of and experience in the present. This is the part of our mind that is the boss and governs how we intentionally behave in the moment.
- *Subconscious mind.* The thoughts, memories, and feelings that are just below what we are present and aware of that could be retrieved by the conscious mind and affect our behavior in the moment. Many of our daily habits reside here. It is important to note that what is in our subconscious mind is not repressed or buried.
- *Unconscious mind.* This is the storehouse of thoughts, memories, and feelings that are repressed or buried and are outside of what

we are consciously aware of. The contents of the unconscious mind include painful, embarrassing, and unpleasant memories and feelings that affect our behavior and generate automatic responses to certain triggers we experience throughout our day-to-day interactions.

We believe much of the battle to mindshift and change behavior lies in an ability to become aware of how the unconscious mind is affecting behavior in the present moment and use the conscious mind to choose actions and thoughts based on this expanded awareness. The unconscious mind can reach back many years (all the way to our childhood) and be so emotionally charged that it is beyond the scope of coaching. Sometimes, therapy or other professional support is needed to help explore its impact. Not being aware of unconscious influences can be a barrier to our ability to mindshift.

When I returned to the company in 2014, my goal was to help Malitta continue to restructure the company. I also wanted to repair the damage to my relationship with her. I was confident we could produce our secret sauce again. I thought the sauce would just have to be used in a different dish, so to speak, since the federal government's small business contracting rules wouldn't allow us to compete for contracts in the conference and events industry we had thrived in. This was part of the transition plan we were implementing when I left the company. We knew we had to shift our primary market focus. Malitta had done a great job after I left of winning contracts that could serve as the foundation for the transition. In addition, we added a sizable multiyear contract win after I returned.

But with respect to our marriage, major damage had been done because I had not kept my word and hadn't returned to the business sooner. This was a promise I had made to her, that I would return to the company if needed. I broke that promise. The hurt and mistrust affected our relationship. That realization and seeing the residual pain I caused began to take a toll on me. One thing that really bothered me was seeing the empty office space—a result of the difficult layoffs Malitta had needed to execute in my absence. Every day I came to the office, I had to face what I'd done. I hated walking through the office and seeing empty cubicles that were filled with people when I left the company. Even writing about it makes me a bit queasy.

My guilt for having been so mindless and egocentric when I left the company infected my thinking. I became fixated on the mistake I had made and the challenges it caused for my marriage and our business. This led me to worry about the future and experience pain. My problems compounded in this pain body existence I was living in. My focus on the past and future instead of the present negatively affected my ability to focus on the tasks that needed to happen in the *now*. We were in rough seas, and I was so focused on the wreckage behind and the waves ahead that I wasn't steering my personal ship very well.

This error thinking was the essence of the law of mind action. This law is defined as "thoughts held in mind produce after their kind."[3] From guilt and regret to self-doubt and uncertainty, I was bringing to me exactly what I was trying to avoid. This was happening when I was still blind, before I heard the words in church—*state of suffering* and *state of harmony*—that kicked off my introspection. When I took a journey within, it was clear to me the power our minds and thoughts can have on our attitudes and perspectives and how the universe responds to us. Depending on who you talk to, this law of mind action can be explained spiritually or logically, but regardless of how it is delivered, it is real. I happen to subscribe to both the spiritual and the logical. Let me explain why.

After my *aha* moment in church, from a spiritual perspective, I adopted a philosophy I learned reading the book *Feel the Fear . . . and Do It Anyway* by Susan Jeffers. Jeffers refers to the "higher self," that place in us where positive thoughts are generated and sent—if we so choose—to our conscious mind, which produces conscious action. The problem is that there is another force that competes to control our thoughts and actions called the "chatterbox." This is the loud and pacing force that is yakking at us, sending the most negative thoughts it can to our conscious mind.[4]

The more the chatterbox wins the battle, the more everything looks like a problem and the less energy we muster to deal with it. And worse yet, our perspective becomes skewed, and we become unable to take what looks like an obstacle and transform it into an opportunity. After the negative thoughts from the chatterbox surface, if we don't filter them out, they get sent to our subconscious mind, where they are easily accessible by the conscious mind to affect behavior.

If we don't develop the skills to filter out the negative thoughts before they get to our subconscious mind, we send messages of fear, scarcity, hopelessness, and doubt to the universe. Guess what we get back? You got it: bad things. On the more logical side of things, these negative thoughts sap our energy, creativity, courage, and talent to a point where our effort and performance are affected in ways that bring what we don't want. So, either way, spiritually or logically, we end up attracting to ourselves what we don't want.

After I began my self-introspective journey, a number of things aligned in my life that helped me learn and understand this way of thinking. Every Sunday, I was getting filled with lessons at church and through my self-study at home. Although these metaphysical teachings certainly are Christian in origin, they are sometimes referred to as "practical Christianity" teachings that are (to me) more actionable than what I had typically experienced in prior churches I attended.

I learned to focus more on taking the "right action" to manifest my desires. More importantly, though, I learned that a higher power resides inside each and every one of us as a source of strength and guidance—that we are the co-creators of our lives with the power of choice, attraction, energy, and action. I was learning that prayer is a time to give gratitude and ask for blessings over my family, friends, and people who are in need. But I was also being taught about meditation and how it is the space where answers are born, where I connect to the spirit inside me and generate divine thoughts and ideas. I have now become a firm believer that to develop the type of connection we want to any higher power, we must both meditate and pray.

This connection to a higher power, or the spirit inside us, is a powerful tool in helping us know when we know—getting confirmation from another source when we aren't sure if we are making the right decision or taking the right course of action. When we are unsure, we can feel alone in making tough calls. When we have a strong, consistent, and ongoing relationship with a higher power in the form of our higher self, we feel much less alone. This connection is what becomes the anchoring source of confidence. And over time, as we experience the reality of how the higher self, conscious mind, subconscious mind, and the universe work in unison, our trust in the relationship grows, we rely on it more, and we make decisions that attract to us the good that we want. We develop true intuition, not just a gut feeling or a hunch but a knowing that comes from our connection and access to our higher self.

> **When we have a strong, consistent, and ongoing relationship with a higher power in the form of our higher self, we feel much less alone.**

Malitta had been on this journey for several years, and I was just beginning. She had a prayer room in our house where she had books—about Christianity, metaphysics, Buddhism, and more—piled up. She wanted to expand her spiritual understanding and connection. As my journey became clearer to me, I realized I needed a place in that prayer room, too. So I asked her if I could share her space. There I collected my own set of books. I even started my own journal, where I chronicled the ups and downs of the ride I was taking. But something else divine and beautiful happened in that room. We began praying and meditating together.

I must admit that, at times, meditation has been tough for me. My mind races, and sometimes the chatterbox finds its way into my thoughts. A few things have helped me with this. One is that even if we can't stop our runaway thoughts, we can try to slow them down so that there is space in between them—a space where those divine, creative, and loving ideas can fit. I have also learned that if I constantly give gratitude and thanks during my meditation, it is very difficult for fear and anxiety to sneak in. I express gratitude for all the small things that happened to me the day before and that will happen in the day unfolding, such as waking up in the morning.

Meditation happens in different forms for different people. A big part of meditation is focus. By focusing, we get still in the present moment. So activities that require focusing on something in the present can be meditative. This is why, when meditating, we are told to focus on our breathing and to return to breathing when our mind wanders. This focus on the present allows us to stop thinking about things behind or ahead of us, those places that allow the chatterbox to use fear, anxiety, and worry to block our connection to positive energy, creativity, and the higher self. By focusing on our breathing and eliminating the chatterbox, we create space to get thoughts and guidance from our higher self that can't get through to our mind when the chatterbox is occupying our mind space.

What other things can we do that require this type of focus? Walking in nature? Other forms of exercise that require mental and physical control? Taking a scenic ride on the Peloton and focusing on the screen in front of you? Sitting quietly (inside or outside) and picking an object to focus our attention on? These are all ways that help us bring our thoughts into the present and chase the fear- and worry-mongering chatterbox out of our mind space. Some of my best insights come when I am on vacation, when I am not constantly getting emails or text messages that can generate chatterbox thoughts to occupy my mind space and push me out of the present. Vacation and travel create space for me to receive insights from higher-self thinking.

Another meditative activity is journaling. This can be especially good for people who have trouble stopping their mind from racing. This practice can help keep us mindful (present) and focused on those things we have identified as important to our joy and success. For a simple journaling practice, please refer back to the My Morning BAGELS exercise at the end of chapter 8.

• • •

The alignment of what I was learning on Sunday, together with the daily reading, prayers, and meditation at home, helped me shift my mindset from *participating* in the experiences that were causing me pain and fear to *observing* myself and my circumstances, identifying opportunities, and then creating the space to suggest to my participant self different ways of thinking and being to act on those opportunities. As an observer, I was able to imagine three people sitting in the room: me, the ally, and the chatterbox. This helped me see how I was listening to the chatterbox and ignoring the ally—that source of positive and supporting thoughts—and how I was focusing on the obstacles and not the opportunities available to me.

When I was able to slow down my thoughts and replace the negative, fear-driven thinking with more optimistic energy, I could see opportunities. After I spent time in the prayer room, I saw an opportunity for me to evolve, grow, and transform into someone who could not only observe my present behavior in the moment but also look back on my past behavior and recognize the lessons I needed to take from it. This observation allowed me to focus less on Malitta and more on my transformation.

PROVE IT LESSON

Making the shift from a participant to an observer can lift us over obstacles and reveal opportunities we have not seen or experienced before. When we can stop experiencing the feelings of our current life circumstances and instead observe what is happening, we can see things differently. This new vantage point helps us to transform ourselves and our behavior.

PROVE IT QUESTIONS

- What would I suggest to someone else if I was observing them living the same painful or undesirable experience that I am in right now?
- What do I see about myself when I shift from participant to observer?
- How would I change my past and future behavior using what I have learned from my new, observer vantage point?

PROVE IT MINDFUL PRACTICES

- Take yourself out of the location and environment where you are experiencing what you don't want. This may be going on a vacation, taking a long walk, or sitting in a different room in your house. It can be difficult for you to be an observer when you are *in* the situation you want to observe.
- Name the person you are when you are participating in the situation rather than observing it. For example, naming myself Ego-Driven Brad triggers me to stop so I can watch it as if I were someone else.
- Once you make the shift from participant to observer, think about how you would advise or coach the participant (e.g., Ego-Driven Brad) on how they should act or behave in the current situation. You can also do this with past actions or behaviors.

CHAPTER 11

VICTIM TO VALOR

> Until we have seen someone's darkness, we don't really know who they are. Until we have forgiven someone's darkness, we don't really know what love is.
> —MARIANNE WILLIAMSON, *ILLUMINATA*

AS I OBSERVED MYSELF LIVING in a state of suffering, it became clear that Malitta had to release me from my victimhood by releasing herself from hers. As she explains in chapter 4, she had to move from victim to valor. She had to kill the pain she felt from my failure to keep my word and put my family first when I didn't return to the company. If she was a victim, I was a victim. Obviously, this was very delicate. I asked her many times why we couldn't just bury the past and move forward. I believed that by keeping me focused on my abandonment, she wasn't allowing me to live in the present. When I told her this, it made things worse. Why? Because she refused to bury her hurt, knowing that if she did, she wouldn't be true to herself. She would just be doing what had gotten us in this situation in the first place: giving me what I needed instead of giving herself what she needed. At the time, I couldn't see I was doing this again.

But Malitta, as you recall, was my mirror. She showed me that I was putting myself first again. This was quite a pill to swallow, given that I had already taken total responsibility for my mistake. I thought that when I accepted the blame, the mirror wouldn't reflect more of the same shortcomings to me. But sometimes we must see a consistent pattern in our behavior before we truly grasp how much something bad has consumed us. Once again, the egocentric side of ego, which generates self-centeredness, was looking back at me. Ego, that same demon that got us where we were in the first place, was still there, just not as obvious.

The reflection was strong and clear. I received the message: I had to stop putting myself first by trying to make Malitta move forward before she was ready and able. Malitta needed to talk about the three-year period of isolation when I was away from the company and the feelings of betrayal and anger that had been created. But when she talked about the past and the mistakes I made, I'd slip into a negative state—and I wanted to move away from that to a place where I could live with myself. So I tried forcing her to move forward with me.

This realization made me conscious of my unconscious habit of protecting myself. For example, when Malitta would remind me that she had to make difficult decisions in my absence and how that made her feel, I didn't want to talk about it. Why? Because it was a thorn taking me back to the fact that I had abandoned her. That made me feel terrible and started the chatterbox, feeding me negative thoughts of how badly I had messed up and how our relationship was suffering because of it.

So here we were, Malitta wanting to face the music, deal with the abandonment head-on, and talk about it so she could accept it and move on. And there I was, wanting to forget about it so my present would not be haunted by my past. During this time, Malitta made it clear that she refused to simply bury what she had experienced and ignore the hurt it caused so we could just move on. She wanted to understand it.

But I couldn't begin to explain why I did what I did until I shifted my focus away from the chatterbox, which told me it was okay to want to move on because staying focused on the past would render me ineffective in the present. That was the self-interested me, the one that put me first, before Malitta. As I began to connect to my higher thoughts and accept the fact that I was being self-centered, I started to see the light. It became clear that I needed to put what she needed first, so she could fully leave her victimhood behind and release me from mine.

We had to go through it, not around it like I wanted. The irony was that to do this, I had to first forgive myself so I could accept talking about it. To succeed, I couldn't beat myself up. Part of what helped me was understanding that it was not my true self that made the mistake. It was the result of some of the "stink" that had gotten on me in life. It was Ego-Driven Brad.

We had to go through it, not around it like I wanted.

The true me didn't have ego and insecurity issues—those issues are negative qualities I picked up along the way, exacerbated by the void left when both my parents died while I was in college. Life experiences have a way of making this happen to all of us. We aren't born with a need for acceptance, anger, jealousy, judgment, fear, insecurity, and so on. We pick up these thoughts and feelings just by living. In fact, I believe we were put on this Earth with exactly what we need to carry out our life's purpose, but the stink we pick up day to day begins to block us from the light and potential of our true self.

After shifting to being an observer, I was able to face what I had done. Then I was able to develop a mantra to be more supportive of Malitta's healing. I started asking myself the question: What is the loving thing to do? This mindfulness habit shifted my focus from protecting myself to putting her and her needs first. I could see this in the observer role. I shifted from a defensive posture to a protective posture. I wanted to stop defending myself and instead protect Malitta. I was becoming more self-aware. I changed the direction in which I was walking.

As Marianne Williamson explains in *A Return to Love*, there are two directions we can walk in: love or fear.[1] I had been walking toward fear—fear of my mistakes and the suffering that resulted. I wanted to run and hide from it. But as long as I ran, it was always going to be there, almost like part of my body. By letting down my defenses and being willing to put Malitta first, I turned in the direction of love. That was the true me. The Brad who came here with the capacity to have compassion and caring beyond myself. The more I walked toward love, the more the chatterbox was silenced and the more the fear-laden thoughts subsided. Just like a bully, the chatterbox doesn't want us to fight back, but the more we fight, the less we get bullied.

Over time, Malitta began to believe I was trying to *help her* move forward and that I was willing to do what she needed to get there. This did two things. First, it helped her complete the process of letting go of her own victimhood. Second, it allowed her to begin to release me from my regret by treating me less and less as the perpetrator and more as a friend who needed her support. My focus on transforming myself got me the forgiveness I had wanted and tried to get before. As this happened, my pain body showed up less and less. I will never forget the day when she put in my hand a bookmark given out at her father's funeral with his favorite scripture, 2 Corinthians 5:17, "Therefore if any man be in Christ, he is a new creature: old things are passed away; behold all things are become new." That was my get-out-of-jail card! I felt released. Bye-bye, pain body.

• • •

I have written here a lot about being released from victimhood. A great feeling indeed. If you have never been a victim, I hope you never will be. Not likely though. At some point, we all experience some bad thing that could cause us to begin feeling sorry for ourselves. Something that calls in our pain body. No matter how much we do or don't deserve that pain body experience, how we deal with it becomes a choice. Pain is inevitable, but suffering is a choice. Making the choice not to be a victim is step one. The next step is to shift from victim to valor.

In chapter 4, Malitta describes the valor—courage in the face of threat or danger—that she displayed in facing the challenges I left her with. To complete my shift away from victimhood, I had to display my own brand of valor. I had to focus on the strength of mind needed to be brave and fight the battle. To do this, I had to train and be prepared to win the battle. I had to "train" to change direction and walk toward love. It didn't happen overnight. I had to develop a routine that got me ready to compete, ready to display valor. I had to change my thinking and my bad habits. I had to get the stink off me. I had to develop new habits that pointed me toward love every day.

So I developed a training regimen to go along with my meditation—a set of habits designed to get me ready for battle and to move from victim to valor. Admittedly, the process wasn't deliberate at first, but the more I made the turn from fear to love, the more deliberate it became. I realized how important it was to develop what I now refer to as bulletproof habits. I picked them up from several places (church talks, books, and articles about mindfulness). The beauty was that I was getting the same message from multiple sources: I had to change my habits. I learned to refer to this as synching; it is no coincidence when we receive the same message from different places. This is a message the universe is sending to us, and we best pay attention. When we pay attention to the message, we strengthen the relationship we have with our higher self. In doing so, I learned to know what I know. The experience of things synching is confirmation we are heading in the right direction.

The message that was reinforced for me more than anything else was that I needed to start off every day generating positive energy and thoughts. I needed to feed myself positivity and operate in a field of positive energy. First, I stopped watching the news when I woke up in the morning or when I couldn't sleep at night. So much of what is in the news and media is fear-provoking and negative. It is not what you want to feed into your consciousness first thing in the morning or in the middle of the night when you already can't sleep. Those news feeds helped keep me pointed toward fear. That was not the direction I needed to walk in.

I replaced the time that I used to spend listening to negativity with sitting in our prayer room alone—sometimes I wrote in a journal, sometimes I read, and sometimes I wrote daily thoughts in my phone that at one point I posted to social media. For many years before I left the company, I sent an email called "Thought for the Week" to employees, and I envisioned myself returning to that habit I loved. These habits gave me positive energy.

I, like Malitta, came to the understanding that nobody was coming to save me. I had to save myself. Now, I could get some help, but getting on my knees, praying, and (what I now call) begging God for divine intervention was not going to result in anything until I committed to taking the right action—action that came from a place of purpose and not pain. Action that came from love and not fear. Action that was driven by the higher power of God outside me *and* within me.

I added other bulletproof habits as well. Exercise, breaking a sweat first thing in the morning, had great benefits both physically and mentally. Physically, I lost weight. I changed my diet by eliminating as much salt and sugar as I could. My goal became to get my ideal weight within the guidelines for my BMI so my doctor would remove "overweight male" from my medical record. That is something I wanted for me. Nobody knew that note was in my medical record, but I did. Mentally, exercise produces the feel-good hormone dopamine. We crave dopamine to make us feel good. It can come from many different sources, some of them not so healthy, like drugs and alcohol. I learned that I needed to get my dopamine shot from morning exercise. Exercise—part of my MEDS (see chapter 9)—not only produced dopamine but also increased my serotonin levels. This helped me feel good *and* pause to accept and act on Malitta's feedback.

I do drink socially, but I am now conscious of the risk of using drinking as self-medication, as opposed to a moderate social activity. When I was walking in fear and uncertainty, alcohol provided me with dopamine, and it helped keep my mind from racing. It was self-medication, but it was the wrong medicine. The right medicine is the right action, and my new MEDS were helping me take it. Right action was coming to save me.

Forgiving myself and implementing new daily habits paved the road from victim to valor. Having valor in the face of possibly losing what mattered most allowed me to shift my mindset from one of needing to be saved to one of saving myself. This was a key for me in committing to taking right action instead of inaction.

PROVE IT LESSON

Walking toward love means walking toward the ally and away from the chatterbox. My walk toward love led me to Malitta's forgiveness and my forgiveness of myself.

PROVE IT QUESTIONS

- In this situation I am in right now, what would it look like to walk toward love and away from fear?
- How can I display love by pausing, being present, and answering the question: What is the loving thing to do?

- Am I brave enough to actually do what comes to me as the answer to that question?

PROVE IT MINDFUL PRACTICES

- Cut off sources of negative energy, especially first thing in the morning. Don't let negativity set the tone for your day.

- Try to start every day by reading something, writing something, and moving—even if it is only ten minutes of each, try to do all three. This trinity starts your day with positive energy.

- Develop mantras you can commit to memory that can shift your mindset and behavior quickly. For example, "What is the loving thing to do?" makes me an observer of that other guy, Ego-Driven Brad. "Nobody is coming to save me" turns me away from my pain body and reminds me to walk toward love.

CHAPTER 12

EGO IMBALANCE TO EGO CONSCIOUSNESS

Ego is the enemy.
—RYAN HOLIDAY, *EGO IS THE ENEMY*

"**FINDING YOURSELF IS NOT REALLY** how it works. You aren't a ten-dollar bill in last winter's coat pocket. You are not lost. Your true self is right there, buried under cultural conditioning, other people's opinions, and inaccurate conclusions you drew as a child and adult that became your beliefs about who you are. 'Finding yourself' is returning to yourself. An unlearning, an excavation, a remembering who you were before the world got its hands on you."[1]

This is a quote from Emily McDowell. It really grabbed my attention because this is exactly what I learned during my struggle to get the stink off me. It was an unlearning, an excavation to return from the ego-based me to the real me.

In chapter 8, I explain what a big part ego played in my stupid decision to leave the company. In chapter 9, I describe how I became aware that ego was my issue. In this chapter, I focus on the process I had to go through to reset my ego to a healthy level. This was what I call my excavation.

Before an excavation could begin, I had to be committed to *fixing* my ego problem. To be committed, I had to really understand what ego means. Ego is a person's view of themselves, their self-esteem. It is an idea we create about who and what we are. This idea comes from sources that can be inside us or outside us. As I have discussed, I believe that connection to a higher power resides in each of us. What is outside us is the world's stuff, and this is where we learn to become something other than what is naturally within us.

So where is the best source for us to develop our self-esteem or ego? Right inside us. My view of myself was built on things outside me. Other people's opinions of me, my bank account, my accomplishments. What happened when my ego source became misdirected to things outside me? I clutched onto them because they shaped how I viewed myself.

This misdirection can lead to terrible things, like it did for me. I have shared in detail the crisis I created. At the root of my decision that caused it was a desire to hold on to the things in the world I thought made me (like having a reputation for being smart). Eventually, this led to what I have referred to as the egocentric me (Ego-Driven Brad)—the me who put me first in all decisions I made. Of course, this was the great fear I talk about in this book—that what I was holding on to so tightly would be taken away, which would have been a big blow to my ego. Intuitively, none of us want experiences that make us think less of ourselves.

Once again, let me be clear: I didn't realize any of this when I was doing it. I viewed myself as being a pretty good person who cared about other people. I was generous and willing to share what I had—knowledge, money, whatever. I loaned significant amounts of money to friends and in some cases never got paid back. My view was that if it wasn't going to hurt me, why wouldn't I loan it? But there was a part of my "generosity" that was driven by that outside source of my ego, my perception that people viewed me as a successful guy who had money. So, when they came to me for money, it fed my ego. To put it simply, although I thought I was helping by loaning them money, unconsciously I was also feeding my ego.

Ego issues show up for most of us. The question is whether ego's existence has elevated to a level where it becomes a poor source of how we see ourselves. Those of us who are (or become) conscious about ego can recognize it and act to control it. I remember reading an article about a famous actor who refuses to read articles about herself because she didn't want it to go to her head, good or bad. To me, she was not allowing the outside source of ego to overtake her inside source. This is someone who was aware she was ego driven, so she put guardrails in place to keep from driving off the road. This may have been a result of a mindshift to ego consciousness.

So you may be saying to yourself, "Wow, do I make any decisions based on a misdirected ego?" or "Nah, I don't do that." Either way is good because to even contemplate the question is a level of awareness that can help you avoid error-based decisions or drifting into a sense of self-importance. As I have thought about this paradigm many times over the last few years, I have asked myself questions like these: Am I exercising, eating right, and trying to lose weight to improve my health, *or* am I doing it to influence what other people think of me? Am I donating money to my friend's charity because I don't want them to be offended if I don't *or* because it is really in my heart to do so? Am I not being more transparent with my friends about the transformation our business went through because I don't think it is necessary for them to know that much about my personal business *or* because I don't want them to change their view of me?

I went through the mindshift of becoming ego aware. So then what? Excavation, baby! I had to start digging to get back to my truer self. Here is the thing: When you start to excavate, you must choose the site to be excavated. Choose the wrong site, and you might never find what you are looking for.

This reminds me of a story Wayne Dyer shared in his book, *You'll See It When You Believe It*, about a man who had his keys in his hands while standing in his house. Suddenly, the power in his house goes out and everything gets pitch black. The man drops his keys and then kneels on the floor feeling unsuccessfully for his keys. He looks out the window and sees that the streetlights are on. So he goes outside under the streetlight and starts looking for the keys. His neighbor comes up and starts helping him, to no avail. After a few minutes, the neighbor asks him where he dropped his keys, and the man says he dropped them in the house. The neighbor asks the man why he is looking for his keys outside and not in the house where he dropped them. The man says he is looking outside because this is where the light is.[2]

> **When you start to excavate, you must choose the site to be excavated. Choose the wrong site, and you might never find what you are looking for.**

Of course, this story shows that the issue was inside, in the darkness, but the man went outside to a light source that could not solve his problem. When we begin to excavate, we must be willing to bring light (awareness) into our darkness. Often, this is where we find our true self—in the dark beneath the dirt that needs to be excavated.

This can be a place where we don't want to go. Maybe we like the feeling we get living from our ego-based self. Maybe we are afraid of what we will find. Maybe we just have no idea how to turn the lights on. Whatever the case, it is incumbent upon us to ask ourselves a big question: Is an excavation needed? There are signs. My signs were clear.

I was living in a state of suffering. I couldn't focus on what was happening in the present—the time that mattered most in creating a different tomorrow—because I was lamenting my past unconscious decision and its ripple impact. In essence, life was no longer working out as it had before, and I was the reason. There was no one else to blame. I felt like my trajectory was heading in the wrong direction—not a good feeling to have in my mid-fifties.

When I was in the success zone, which I had experienced for much of my life, I visualized a carefree life by age sixty, one where my main focus would be helping my sons have the experiences they wanted. I envisioned having achieved everything I wanted and helping entrepreneurs and business leaders successfully develop and achieve their dreams and purpose. But this was not the path my reality was taking me. There were balls in the air and questions on the table that didn't have to exist. I had put my vision in jeopardy, so I knew I needed to make a change.

As I groped in the darkness to feel for my own keys, I realized I was excavating the wrong site! I was just like the man Wayne Dyer described; I was shining the light in the wrong place. Instead of doing a dig on myself, I was trying to excavate the sites of people around me.

Most notably, I was digging on Malitta's site. Imagine, you find the courage to excavate your own site and here comes someone else who starts digging your site, too. Instead of focusing on myself, I was digging to help Malitta rediscover *her* true self. I needed her to hurry up and find herself (find peace) so she would do what I wanted her to do: let me off the hook by releasing me from the role of perpetrator, as I explain in an earlier chapter.

We can't excavate someone else's site; we can only excavate our own. The journey into and beyond ourselves is a personal one. It requires us to identify and face the blockages that created the version of us that developed as we adapted and gave into the world's view of us. We have to get the stinky life experiences off us that aren't serving us well.

So, what did my excavation look like? It was really an exercise of becoming mindful, which is being present, conscious, and aware.

Becoming Present

For me, so much of my mind space was being taken up by limiting chatterbox thoughts. I could not stop looking behind me at the mindless mistakes I made. I had to bring my thoughts into the present, the here and now, where my ability to act today affects what happens in the future. I needed a mindshift.

This started with becoming intellectually and spiritually aware of how the world works. As I have mentioned, I did this through a combination of practices that allowed me to understand the power that my mind and my thoughts have on my actions in the present, which drive my future. Once I incorporated this into my consciousness, I began to focus more on the *now* and started to rediscover my true self. I understood that getting hit with the two-by-four (the fallout from my decision to leave the company) was actually one of the best things that ever happened to me. It forced me to see my ego source was in the wrong place, and I had to redirect it. This changed the way I experience life in ways I hadn't imagined.

My excavation into the present also included understanding and memorizing the twelve powers from the book *The Twelve Powers of Man* by Charles Fillmore.[3] Here is how I understand and use them:

- Imagination: The ability to visualize or create options or ideas
- Understanding: To know, perceive, and comprehend
- Will: The ability to decide and act
- Zeal: To be enthusiastic, to motivate
- Faith: The ability to believe that something will happen that has not happened yet
- Power: The ability to regulate and dominate
- Love: The ability to attract and unify
- Judgment: The ability to look at things from different perspectives
- Order: The ability to organize and adjust

- Strength: The ability to stabilize and persevere
- Release: The ability to eliminate what does not serve me well
- Life: The ability to give birth to what serves me well

I looked at the twelve powers like a tool kit I could reach into and pick up whichever tool I needed in the moment to deal with whatever was happening. I came to understand these abilities as sources of power inside me that are given to all of us when we are born. But here is the most important thing: I had to be *present* to remember the twelve powers were at my disposal and to access them whenever I needed.

In other words, as my understanding of how the world works developed, I had to be more present to practice what I was learning. I had to stay conscious.

Becoming Conscious

I define being conscious as a state of positive, deliberate, and complete thinking. This is a place where we make decisions and take action not affected by emotions, blind spots, fixed mindsets, and of course, ego. For the sake of brevity, I will call these light blockers.

To become conscious, I had to be self-aware. If conscious thinking must be unencumbered by light blockers, then I must know what my light blockers are and accept them. In his book *The Seven Spiritual Laws of Success*, Deepak Chopra calls out defenselessness, acceptance, and responsibility.[4] I have committed these words to memory because for me to reach a level of self-awareness, I had to not be defensive (one of the Four Horsemen I discussed earlier) when my mirror (Malitta) pointed out my light blockers to me. I had to accept them as being true, and I had to be responsible for removing them or at least controlling them.

I also had to learn, understand, and remember the opposite state of being conscious: unconsciousness. I have described this as the autopilot part of our mind—the part of our mind that takes over when we aren't present and focused on the now and doesn't give space for us to access tool kits like the twelve powers. Acting unconsciously is like your mind's autopilot using the light blockers you have picked up over the years to dictate your actions and behaviors rather than you acting in the light from your true (excavated) self.

Becoming Aware

Awareness comes in three parts: self-awareness, environmental awareness, and intellectual awareness. Self-awareness helps me not lie to myself and accept responsibility for my light blockers. For example, when I became aware of and accepted my ego challenges, I was able to manage them better and make fewer unconscious decisions.

Environmental awareness helps me understand what is going on with the people around me, what their needs are, and how I should consider their needs before moving in a certain direction. For example, not staying in the business when I should have. I didn't *understand* as I made that decision that my ego was overriding everything.

The last component of awareness, intellectual awareness, helps me understand what is going on in the big picture so I can connect the dots between any decision I am facing and how that decision may result in things I want or don't want.

I had some enlightening discoveries as I excavated myself. Often, we come to understand some of the most interesting facets of ourselves by returning to our childhood. Here is one I found. When I was young, my father would sometimes call me "dummy" when he was trying to teach me something and I wasn't catching on. It could have been something about sports or how to cut the grass, but it was always when he was trying to get me to learn something. I've recognized that I get a positive energy shot when someone calls me smart and that I like knowing stuff and will often go down rabbit holes learning things. I also like to teach people what I know. During my excavation, I realized that my desire to be "smart" is possibly linked back to the frequency with which my father called me a dummy when I was having trouble learning the things he was teaching me. I also realize my desire to know stuff and share it with others may be related to my sensitivity to being a better teacher than my father was.

This story is a good example of how self-awareness, intellectual awareness, and environmental awareness work together to create ego consciousness. The awareness of what gives me self-esteem, where it comes from, and how it affects my interactions with others and the decisions I make. First, I discovered something about myself (self-awareness that I like to know things), and then I came to understand why I am the way I am (intellectual awareness that I wanted to be viewed as smart). I completed the awareness trifecta when I became aware of how this need to be smart and desire to share what I know affects the people around me (environmental awareness). One of Malitta's uncles, who I spend a fair amount of social and leisure time with, told her that although he is fond of me, I sometimes come off as a know-it-all when I start sharing books I have read and what I have learned. Malitta wasn't really supposed to tell me what he said, but, as my mirror, she did. She thought I should know (to help my growth mindset). When I thought about it, I could see his point. I needed to chill out on some of the sharing and teaching I was doing. So I made a change. It's not that I never share anymore, but I am much more aware of *when* I do it (which is less often) and *how* I do it (in a less "teachy" manner, often asking questions and listening to people talk about their experiences and knowledge rather than only sharing mine).

Needless to say, I also realized that getting positive self-esteem from people calling me smart was an example of my getting my ego source from outside me. The key here is that now I understand that, and although it has not been completely eliminated, my awareness of it helps me not be manipulated and fall prey to people who know they can get something from me if they call me smart (partly how I ended up taking that job!).

Although this childhood story sounds harsh, my father did not intend any harm when he called me a dummy. I know based on the love he showed me that he did not understand how he was affecting my ego sensitivities. He was not self-aware, environmentally aware, or intellectually aware of how his teaching style was creating experiences that would shape who I was both positively (I like to learn) and negatively (seeking self-esteem/approval outside me).

My excavation revealed the root of most evil for me was ego. By now, you are probably clear that I believe ego imbalance happens when our ego source is in the wrong place. It is almost like the minute we get here, the world starts teaching us to get our idea of who we are from outside us. This creates several blockages that move us further away from the real us and promotes egocentric (self-centered) and/or egotistical (self-important) behaviors. We can find ourselves beholden to forces outside us, forces we can't control that can have us making error decisions.

Ego might not be your issue. But you must ask yourself: Is there some issue that is blocking me from my true self? It may be insecurity, jealousy, shame—the list goes on. Then you must ask yourself if an excavation is in order. If there is too much pain or trauma to do it on your own, you might need help from a mental health professional. It may be an extensive excavation or a short dig, but if we want true joy and a great life, we must do it. When I excavate (this is an ongoing practice), I am in touch with the real me: creative, kind, loving, beautiful, expansive, abundant, and receptive (words I have memorized from Wayne Dyer's *The Power of Intention*).

A few years ago, I brought home a rock I found at a beach while on vacation. I spray-painted the rock purple and wrote those seven words on it. I keep it in our prayer room, and every now and then, I pick it up and hold it in both hands as a mindful practice to remember who I am.

PROVE IT LESSON

We are a combination of who we were when we came into this world *and* our life experiences that have affected us and shaped our view of ourselves. This adaptation may have caused us to live from the outside in, allowing the opinions and expectations of people and things outside us to drive our decisions and how we view ourselves. When this happens, we aren't in control of our actions and behavior; others are. This is the time for us to excavate and get the "stink" off us that has accumulated. A return to our true self.

PROVE IT QUESTIONS

- Where is my ego source—inside me or outside?
- Does my sense of ego have me feeling self-important or unimportant?
- How does this affect my relationships and decisions?
- If ego isn't my issue, is there something else about me, right now, that needs to be excavated to get back to my true self?

PROVE IT MINDFUL PRACTICES

Daily journaling is so important that I'm recommending it again here. It is one of the most important and simplest tactics we can use on our journey within. It forces us to be present, *and* we are more likely to commit to (and not forget) what we write down. The My Morning BAGELS format (see chapter 8) is a great tool because it pushes us to set small goals, reflect on them, and learn from our experiences. All of this supports the self-awareness that is the foundation of ego consciousness and personal transformation overall.

Additionally, read or listen to books or other sources that both teach and remind you what you already know. Chapter 8 discusses the concept of a fixed versus a growth mindset. To move from an outside to an inside ego source, we must have a growth mindset and be willing to learn new things and make changes based on what we learn. Reading keeps our mind open and keeps us growing. In personal transformation, what we let into our minds is equally important to what we release or keep out of our minds. In fact, what we let in fills the space we clear when we move from mind full to mindful.

The following is a list of books that had a profound impact on me:

- *The Seven Spiritual Laws of Success* by Deepak Chopra
- *Feel the Fear . . . and Do It Anyway* by Susan Jeffers
- *Breaking the Habit of Being Yourself* by Joseph Dispenza
- *Ego Is the Enemy* by Ryan Holiday
- *Emergence* by Derek Rydall
- *The Power of Intention* by Wayne Dyer
- *The Untethered Soul* by Michael Singer

CHAPTER 13

INSECURITY TO INNER PEACE

> Every one of us has a *why*, a deep-seated purpose, cause or belief that is the source of our passion and inspiration.
> —SIMON SINEK, *FIND YOUR WHY*

THE EXCAVATION PROCESS IS HELPFUL both in its result of reconnecting us with who we really are and in getting rid of what blocks us from it. This was important for me because one of my biggest blockages was living in angst because of what I had done. As I have shared, we all have fears, but it is how we choose to manage fears that can make or break us. For example, if fear paralyzes us, then we are, well, paralyzed—frozen in place, unable to take the actions needed to move us forward, which essentially moves us further away from the direction we want to go.

This can generate unproductive thinking that leads to poor decisions. Fear can block our connection to the pure potential that exists in all of us—the connection to all we need to do anything we want. Any way we look at it, fear and our mismanagement of it is bad news and one of the greatest threats to living up to our potential. This may cause us to leave our dreams on the table. But the excavation allows us to identify fear and face it, explore it, and manage it. Then we can begin to make better decisions and take better actions. It is almost as if the shovel gets bigger as the digging happens, allowing us to go in deeper and faster.

Fear can also lead to insecurity, causing us to not step out of the box to follow the flow of life and where it takes us. Insecurity makes us afraid to deviate from what we know and afraid to stop doing things we know aren't working—because we don't know what else we will do if we stop. This is what drives busy work. It's the chatterbox telling us that if we stop what we are doing, we will fail because we aren't working ourselves to death.

This is error thinking at its worst. It gives power to outside forces that can drive our decisions. It's, for example, asking what other people will think if you downsize your office and staff. It's an unwillingness to release your attachment to money (or something else) to create a future that is better. It's being afraid to stop what you are doing and ask yourself what you desire and why. All this error thinking keeps us busy, either swimming hard, unsure if we're headed in the right direction because we have not stopped to *decide* where we want to go, or allowing currents to take us along because we are too afraid to swim against them.

For people who don't have issues managing their insecurities, this might not make sense. But believe it or not, sometimes we don't want to know if we are moving further from our own shore because, if we do know, then we have to figure out what else we should be doing and make a change. Making that change can be scary, requiring us to face things that might make us more insecure. So we stay in place ignoring the harm we are doing to ourselves (and people around us) because we are afraid to change. It's not rational. But that's how powerful insecurity and fear can be.

Let me tell you how fear affected me. When I finally kept my promise and returned to the company, I had a fear of letting Malitta down again—in my mind that would have resulted in more challenges in our relationship and the business. I came back to the company with a new knowledge base related to health care. I had learned a great deal during the three years I was away, so that, coupled with our company's twenty-plus years of experience working with public health programs, positioned us to help private physicians prepare for and implement a wellness program under new health care laws. Many smaller physician practices didn't have the internal resources to provide the newly available services to patients, but they could outsource and expand services to their patients and gain additional revenue. This opportunity for us was to be an outsource partner to doctors. So we waded into the water of developing this service offering. We invested a lot of time, effort, and money.

It was the right decision because in a volatile, uncertain, complex, and ambiguous (VUCA) business environment, after you do the research and analyze the numbers, the rule is to try the business idea if it looks viable. Go for it. If it works, great, but if it is going to fail, fail fast and move on. We implemented the business idea, and there were two major challenges: (1) The revenue we were paid for the services, as compared to the labor costs we incurred, resulted in low profit margins, and (2) it was difficult to get patients to sign up for the service so we could deliver and then bill the doctor for it. We knew about the low profit margins from our analysis and planned to offset that with volume. However, the second challenge was unforeseen and largely out of our control—doctors and their staff had to sign up the patients directly. With so many new requirements emerging in the health care environment, it was difficult to get doctors to focus on signing up their patients.

With the low margins *and* low volume, the downward trajectory was clear. Even so, my insecurity kept me in a space of resistance, blocking me from facing reality and taking the right action. We could have made the next decision: to fail fast by shutting down the service once we determined that the volume we needed to be profitable was not realistic. But instead, we stuck with it longer than we should have, keeping our heads down, working harder to make something unworkable work. Why? I had done a lot of work to conceive this idea, I had convinced Malitta it was a good idea, and she put in a lot of work, too. Our son was also involved. He was a certified health coach, and he managed our community health professionals who were delivering the service to the patients. I was the lead for this new project, and I had us wrapped up in this thing—afraid for it not to work. This left me feeling pretty insecure.

One day, our son said to Malitta and me, "If this business is low profit *and* neither of you likes what it's taking to make it work, why are you working so hard and investing so much in it?" His observation was obvious to him but not to me because I was operating in a mindset of fear and letting my attachment to making it work blind me. His words turned on the light, and I recognized the chatterbox in my head was bullying me into not facing reality. That mindshift moment prompted us to push through a couple of tough meetings where we analyzed the numbers and the different possible scenarios before confirming that the probability of success was not likely. We shut it down. I faced my fear of failure and embraced it and that allowed me to take the right action.

But my lights were about to get even brighter. We still had several government contracts that were active and producing profits, but they were not going to last forever. We had the option of continuing in government contracts, but neither Malitta nor I had any interest in gearing back up for that type of grind and existence. We had sold several contracts, and I could see the end of our remaining contracts on the horizon, and that worried me because I hadn't figured out a specific path ahead. To keep the business running, we were going to have to generate more new revenue. We kicked around our options; we were at a strange and unexpected fork in the road. And as time moved on, we found ourselves drifting in and out of conversations about the option of staying in the government contract industry, to keep the business as it had been, or exploring second career options.

Again, our son could see what was happening and served as a mirror to us both. He asked why we would go back and do something we don't like doing. His perspective—that unless we absolutely must, we shouldn't do work we hate, living miserably during the week, waiting for the weekend to live (or work more)—was sinking in. We didn't *have* to do this. We had a choice.

As they say, sometimes the student becomes the teacher. He asked us what we love to do. I added this question to my excavation process and continued the dig to get the stink of fear and ego off the answer. Inspired by the mirror and light our son's question gave me, and with the help of *Emergence* by Derek Rydall, I started journaling and identifying the qualities I had when I achieved success before I started giving in to blockages that led to decisions that were outside in and ego based.

Journaling made me more conscious that I thrive when I motivate, inspire, learn, share, and lead. This all culminated in a personal vision to help others tap into their purpose and potential, living based on what is inside them, not outside. My own experience and journey to recognize, fix, discover, and recover myself have inspired me to help people wake up before a crisis or misery shines its light. I was finding inner peace, a place where insecurity is overwhelmed by a connection to purpose.

I found inner peace in my purpose. As I have mentioned, I was put on this journey to find purpose when my minister's sermon asked whether I was living in a state of pain or a beautiful state of harmony. Insecurity is a place of pain; purpose is a place of harmony. I (re)found my purpose by doing my excavation. I had to go back within myself to find it, back to who and what I am absent of the outside forces that began to melt me like an iceberg in warm water. Notice I said *am* instead of *was*. I didn't stop being me. I didn't have to create a new version of myself—I had to rediscover who I've always been.

When I rediscovered myself I wanted to write about my journey. I wanted to share (1) how I got off track and pointed away from my purpose, (2) the events and circumstances that woke me up, and (3) what I had to do (excavate) to identify the blockages in the way of my getting back to me. Once those blockages were identified, I had to become self-aware and trust a mirror to show me who and what I looked like. The person who created the crisis wasn't the real me, and my mirror (Malitta) showed me that. Once I understood this, I put practices and a regimen in place to strengthen my resolve to overpower the blockages and hone an awareness to recognize them when they show up again—*because they always try to come back.*

The other beautiful thing that happens when we point toward purpose and inner peace is that opportunities present themselves to help us move toward them. Opportunities are always present but sometimes difficult to see when we are pointed toward pain. When we are pointed toward pain, we see obstacles. When we are pointed toward purpose, we see opportunities. This mindshift created a new mindset for me.

> **When we are pointed toward pain, we see obstacles. When we are pointed toward purpose, we see opportunities.**

Here is another story that illustrates this. When we decided to transition out of the large, mostly empty office space, we had a huge number of desks, modular furniture, filing cabinets, desktop and laptop computers, large scale copiers, and so on—in other words, *stuff.* I was reluctant to let go of this stuff because I thought that, one day in the future, we would return to the past. Did you catch that? Return to the past in the future? I was focused on the past and using it to project the future. So Malitta and I decided to put all that stuff in storage (thinking we might need it again someday). We spent a huge amount of time and money inventorying, packing, moving, and storing the stuff. At one point, it was costing us thousands of dollars a month in rent to keep *stuff!*

When we gradually realized we would never use a lot of that stuff again, our first inclination was to sell (rather than give away) what we could. (Somehow the thought of recovering some of the cost soothed and better justified having held onto it all.) Meanwhile, we continued to pay the monthly storage fees. Periodically, we had to go to the storage units to retrieve records or other documents needed for the government contracts we still had. Every time I went to a storage unit and moved stuff to get to the stuff we needed, I experienced *pain*. Every time I saw a charge on the credit card for the storage units, I experienced *more pain*. That stuff pointed my attention to the past, where the pain was, and that created an unnecessary emotional weight.

I needed to turn toward my purpose to see opportunity. We were creating our own obstacles when we held onto the past (our stuff), and that created a focus on pain and insecurity when we should have been fully invested in purpose and opportunity. What happened once I shifted my mindset from pain to purpose?

First, after limited success selling our stuff, we finally donated and trashed almost all of it until we had only one storage unit costing $100 a month. Then, I shifted to a focus on the future, which led me to write this book and apply my skills and passion to help others become their best selves. I moved away from trepidation about the future and toward an inner peace about it, and that shift created opportunities to live out my purpose.

As that inner peace set in, I became less attached to setting goals and relentlessly pursuing them when there were signs and indicators that certain paths were not meant to be. I learned to walk away and not view walking away as quitting. Quitting happens when we are afraid or we are unwilling to put in the work or take a calculated risk to achieve a goal. Walking away is a conscious decision that happens after putting in the work and recognizing when things just aren't coming together; it's about honoring signs that maybe it is time to just stop. This is akin to the failing fast approach.

A seemingly great employment opportunity presented itself just as I opened my mind to new opportunities. Another job was not in line with what Malitta and I had planned as we worked to redirect the company's focus, but I decided to investigate (Malitta and I both had reached a point of being open to redefining—together or apart—how we would live out our purpose). I found that the job opportunity aligned with my experience and the responsibilities were things I enjoyed doing. Fortunately for us, the planning we had done to sell some of the federal contracts we had gave us financial flexibility that allowed us to choose our options. This was a very different situation than when I took the local government appointment in 2010. So Malitta and I discussed it, and *together* we made the decision that I would continue through the job vetting process. We decided that although we were fortunate enough to have the time and resources to focus on what we really love to do, we should keep all our options open and not ignore opportunities that showed up at our door. This was a sign of inner peace. I made it to the final candidate group, and after a few weeks, the recruiter called and told me they decided to fill the position with another candidate.

When I received the news, I was surprised. All signs pointed toward me receiving a job offer. I wasn't sure I was going to take the job, but still, I was disappointed (small remaining traces of an imbalanced ego). Then my higher thoughts kicked in. I thought, *This clearly is not the path for me. This is not meant to be.* So I released it and moved on, knowing a better path was waiting. I went to Malitta and told her that I didn't get the job. I will never forget how she smiled and hugged me; I could see that she could see the new me. She could see my mindshift.

I can't leave it here though because I know you are wondering what happened next. Was there something better out there? Well, yes, but it didn't show up right away. It was about a yearlong journey of learning to allow life to flow to me before a path that aligned with my passion and felt designed for me showed up. During that year of flowing, the company had taken on consulting projects that allowed me to warm up and hone my leadership training and organizational transformation skills. One day I got a phone call out of nowhere from a CEO of a multibillion-dollar company that I had a business relationship with, asking me to dinner to discuss an opportunity. That dinner led to the largest consulting engagement of my career—one that brought together my skills, knowledge, and passion. That was a manifestation of the law of attraction.

Through my journey from insecurity to inner peace, I realized part of the beautiful state of harmony for me is doing what I love to do. For all of us, that true love resides close to our truest self. As I have discussed extensively, life can move us further and further away from our true self and toward the ego self. That is what happened to me. Much of the work I had been doing in my career was work I hadn't enjoyed. I enjoyed parts of it, but a lot of it I did not. This realization caused me to focus my time and attention on expanding the part I love, like learning, sharing, helping others rediscover their own passions, and teaching the power of mindshifting by writing this book.

PROVE IT LESSON

Fear and insecurity feed each other. If we can tackle one the other will fall, too. We have to be aware of what is happening in order to face fear, manage it, and move it out of our way. Once we clear the way, inner peace will settle in as we connect to our purpose, but we must be patient.

PROVE IT QUESTIONS

- What do I love to do? What leaves me feeling positive, upbeat, and optimistic about the future?
- Why don't I pursue more of what I love to do?
- Is fear or insecurity blocking me from pursuing my dreams?

PROVE IT MINDFUL PRACTICES

- Search for purpose. Purpose is where our peace is. Insecurity and fear can't survive in a place of peace. Look for purpose by being aware of what you love to do and being open to what comes your way (hint: it doesn't have to come from your job). The search for purpose is much easier to do when you are present. Purpose and love live in the same place; find one and you will find the other.
- Become aware of activities that generate positive energy and thoughts. For me, it is learning new things. I love learning. When I learn, I feel good about the future and good about myself. Those feelings open my mindset and push negative thoughts out of my mind that block my imagination and creativity.
- Once you activate positive energy and thoughts by doing something you love, your mindset is primed to recognize your purpose and connect to it. For me, my love of learning connects me with purpose. Love and purpose overcome insecurity and fear, which gives us inner peace.

CHAPTER 14

TIP OF THE ICEBERG TO TOP OF THE MOUNTAIN

> But it really doesn't matter with me now, because I've been to the mountaintop. . . . I've seen the Promised Land.
>
> —MARTIN LUTHER KING JR.,
> "I'VE BEEN TO THE MOUNTAINTOP"

ICEBERGS FORM WHEN CHUNKS OF ice break off from glaciers, ice shelves, or a larger iceberg. The largest part of an iceberg is underwater. But what is most relevant to this chapter is the fact that icebergs can melt. When an iceberg reaches warm water, the new climate attacks it from all sides. On the iceberg's surface, warm air melts snow and ice into melt ponds that can penetrate the iceberg and widen cracks. Simultaneously, warm water washes against the iceberg edges, melting the ice and breaking off chunks. Below the surface water, warmer waters melt the bottom of the iceberg.

So, what do we have here? A mass that forms by breaking off from that which created it, with a possibility of melting away. It only takes a small piece of an iceberg to sink massive ships, like the *Titanic*. That is not an existence I want for my life. Eventually, icebergs melt, but before they do, they can cause massive damage to the ships they encounter. And what's worse, a melting iceberg is seemingly attacked from all sides as if the conditions around it have turned against it, destroying it from the outside in.

As I reflect back on my decision to walk out on our company and the tumult that followed, I see I was having what I call an iceberg experience—an existence created from destructive forces outside me. This is what happens when our idea of who we are comes from outside rather than inside—we eventually break off from our home base or higher power, that which created us, and separate, drifting further and further apart from it. When our ego gets in the way of our connection to a higher power, we no longer see ourselves as part of that larger mass. And then, when the circumstances in our life heat up, we start to melt. Soon, it becomes difficult to know ourselves as who we were when we came into this world. And worse yet, the waters that block us from our true self—fear, ego, doubt, judgment, anger, shame, and so on—begin to destroy us. It's the age-old strategy of divide and conquer: separate us from our creator and attack the weaker us.

This sounds like we have been set up, targeted for destruction. But the person who really sets us up is *ourselves*. When we allow outside sources to guide our sense of identity (who we see ourselves as), we separate ourselves and become a victim, melting away into someone we either no longer recognize or don't want to be. Again, as with icebergs, this doesn't happen to everyone, but we are all at risk. We can stop this process by finding our way back to the glacier, the source that created the original us, and reconnecting to it—accessing the power and strength we had when we were part of the larger mass, the universe and higher power that created us. In this metaphor, the meltdown after separation is a crisis, such as the turmoil I created. Remember, enlightenment usually happens after a crisis, but it doesn't have to. It's our choice.

When we allow outside sources to guide our sense of identity, we become someone we either no longer recognize or don't want to be.

We have free will, so we can choose another way. That, to me, is the way of the mountain. A mountain is formed when large pieces of the earth smash together below the ground and force a mass of land to be pushed upward. A mountain (the mass of land that has been elevated) never detaches from what created it; in fact, it is supported by what created it. Mountains can shrink from erosion due to weather, water, and so on. These are the forces of attrition (negative conditions akin to negative thoughts and energy). But mountains can also grow from ongoing underground forces of uplift (akin to positive thoughts and energy).

The mountain experience is very different from the iceberg experience. The mountain might shrink, but because it stays connected to the source that created it, it also has a chance to grow. This is a competition between forces of attrition from what surrounds and happens around it and forces of uplift that come from the mountain's source of creation, its foundation. These forces of attrition can shrink us: everyone experiences fear, ego, doubt, judgment, anger, shame, and other light blockers. Yet there are other forces that lift us: encouragement, love, faith, joy, courage, inner peace, and self-awareness. Working to win this battle displays our valor.

This is clear to me *now*, once I could see that I was living like an iceberg, getting attacked from all sides by the negative forces around me. My crisis led me to lean in to an inbound journey of introspection and excavation that continues today. I continue to find more of what I started digging for, the real me. Not all the dirt and stink have been dug up and cleaned off me, but I am now dealing with it, living in the light instead of darkness, which means I can more easily see the dirt and stink that remain. As I shared before, I manage this through awareness: self-awareness, environmental awareness, and intellectual awareness.

I can't allow the dirt to fall back in and cover me up again. I must continue to understand that in crisis I must have faith, but I also must take right action. No one is coming to save me if I don't first choose to save myself. Mindfulness (being present, conscious, and aware) is my greatest weapon. My daily practice of expressing gratitude, meditating, journaling, exercising, repeating opposition thinking, repeating mantras, visualizing what I desire, and more—these are my bulletproof habits. I am not saying my habits must be your habits, but they have worked for me. You can find what works for you. These habits helped transport me from a melting iceberg to a mountain that I am making larger by staying mindful of forces that can erode me and forces that lift me. On my mountaintop, I create and more often experience what I desire, but as an iceberg, I put myself at risk of melting away as things around me heat up and block the connection to my higher and better self.

I have shared my journey to help you see that success, joy, and abundance are there for you when you dedicate yourself to a purpose that gives you inspiration, courage, faith, and conviction—something that moves you to reconnect to the perfect you that was put here with everything you need inside to have what you want. But you've got to get the stink off that has accumulated through life experiences. Once you brave the journey of introspection, maybe you'll find you don't have to dig very far to get to your true self. Maybe you've managed to keep a lot of life's stink off you. If that's you, *great*! I love it. But if you are not sure or already know you are a melting iceberg, take the journey to your mountaintop (living from within, connected to forces of uplift). It's a much safer place to build your life on and it doesn't have to take a crisis to get you there. I'm here now, climbing to a mountaintop, building a life that is giving me greater joy and peace, a life in which mindfulness and being present in the now are guardrails keeping me moving toward more positive experiences.

As I close this chapter and this part of my journey, I am reminded of remarks I gave at my father's funeral. The last words of those remarks were "Well, Dad, I'm coming to stand by you on the mountaintop and be great." I was a nineteen-year-old college student at Howard University. My parents had been followers of Dr. Martin Luther King Jr. When I was young, they played his speeches around the house. Some have told me that my father, a member of the same fraternity as Dr. King, marched with him. My father used to tell me, "Bradford, you're going to be great one day." These words, together with the admiration and love I knew my father had for MLK, led me to speak about the mountaintop at my father's funeral. As I wrote this chapter, I thought about the words I wrote and spoke as a very young man. A young man who was closer to the real me than I was as a fifty-year-old man. Life experiences and how I dealt with them had made me an iceberg, separated from my source. Those experiences created the egocentric Brad. So I am coming full circle as I journey back to my true self and dust off the connection to my source, aiming for the mountaintop. A place where true greatness awaits all of us.

PROVE IT LESSON

There are good and bad forces when you are on a mountain, but you have a much stronger foundation to handle forces on a mountain than you do as an iceberg. The mountain shows all of itself, where its unique beauty can be seen, while the iceberg hides 90 percent of its existence below the water. Anything that *needs* to be hidden isn't the thing to be trusted as the foundation for an existence. If you feel like you're on an iceberg, get off before it melts.

PROVE IT QUESTIONS

- Am I living like an isolated iceberg or a mindful mountain?
- Am I detaching from my family and friends when life is challenging me?
- When I do get input from others, do I spend more time debating or listening to what I hear?

PROVE IT MINDFUL PRACTICES

Pay attention to signs you may be living like an iceberg:

- You don't get input or other perspectives when you are facing a difficult situation or big decision.
- Insecurity, fear, and other negative thoughts fill the majority of the space in your mind.
- You spend the majority of your time when you are interacting with other people talking rather than listening.
- You find you rarely change your opinion or point of view when working with or interacting with family, friends, and coworkers.
- You avoid getting constructive feedback on how you may be able to improve an aspect of your personal or professional life.
- You develop the majority of your thoughts and perspectives from social media.
- You don't have anyone in your personal life telling you things you don't want to hear.
- You rarely seek to learn new things.

Then take action to move toward a mountaintop existence:

- Become an observer of your own life and answer the question: Am I more of a giver or a taker?
- When giving input or making decisions, give consideration to what is best for others who may be affected.
- Get involved in a volunteer activity or something where you help other people.
- When sharing your thoughts and ideas with other people, listen to their feedback and ask clarifying questions.
- Be sure to have someone in your life who is not afraid to tell you when they think you are wrong or making a mistake.
- Find a source for learning new things and developing new ways of thinking. It could be reading or listening to books, taking online classes, or engaging in conversations with people who don't think like you do.

MALITTA'S EPILOGUE

WHEN I CRIED OUT TO the universe, I didn't expect that the universe would answer me with the highest truth—the one lodged inside me that I wasn't facing and couldn't see as the root cause of my pain. When it seemed I had no one else, I begged for a higher power to rescue me. But I wanted to be rescued by making the chamber of my torture more comfortable to stay in.

It seemed my cries were not being answered, so eventually, I lost my will to fight. In losing my will to fight against the storms I faced, I started to see my entire circumstance from a different lens. This was the answer and a blessing from the universe. I began to see the beauty of all that was unfolding. I had been climbing an old mountain alone that was never going to make me happy. The only happiness I'd known on that mountain had moved on and was not going to return.

But still, I resisted and drifted in an unconscious mindset. For a while, I continued to confuse self-preservation with a form of self-love. Self-preservation is imprisoning. It keeps you locked in and focused on protecting what you've gained and what you have known—things of the past. Preservation is never going to be enough. For me, trying to hold on to and protect the accumulations of life is the best way to weigh myself down—creating burdens that make it hard to move forward.

When pushed down far enough, the void of peace (and joy) creates behaviors that eventually add even more distance between the current and desired state of existence. It can cause pleasure-seeking and misery-soothing habits. Habits like overeating (or eating poorly), drinking more, being overly critical, being defensive and overly sensitive, and living in isolation are just some of the ways my discontent manifested. Some might even develop an overdependence on receiving applause, attention, and recognition—in need of external confirmation to help them fight inner battles of discontent.

These self-soothing strategies not only are temporary but can exacerbate frustration by prolonging the process of dealing with the real issue. The word *enjoyment* has roots back to the 1550s and stems from the Old French word *enjoir*, which has a transitive meaning of "take pleasure in."[1] I choose to take pleasure in how I spend my days, hours, and even minutes. This happens only if I choose to stay conscious about all life has shown me and, in turn, think and act consciously in present moments.

The word *joy* dates back to about 1200 and stems from the Old French word *joie*, which means "to feel pleasure or delight."[2] Current definitions of joy include "a state of happiness; expression or display of glad feeling."[3] Because feelings come from the inside, so must joy. It is inside work. I learned I needed to *choose* to be happy; it wasn't going to miraculously show up in my life because of what I was doing, what I owned, or who was in it. It would arrive in my life when I could make the decision to *be* it. It is something no one can take from me unless I give them permission. Sure, I will have disappointments and hurt, but I still get to be the one to decide if I want to continue being joyful (or not).

The choice is always mine, and the choice is always yours. I've had bad life experiences beyond what was shared in this book. Death, sexual assault, and relationship losses that have hurt and affected me deeply. I always have the choice of carrying my pain about these events by mourning, begrudging, and being angry, but doing that (for me) would be self-sabotage. I would have to sacrifice my joy, and I won't do that.

It isn't always as simple as choosing to be joyful and to focus on good thoughts—some things hurt much too much for that. But I find that with a conscious practice of seeking to feel better, in time I become better.

Making the decision to free myself from the mental algorithms hidden in my subconscious mind from years of relying on external cues and social conditioning led me to the top of a new mountain I otherwise would never have found. I spend my days writing, speaking, and helping others to discover, ascend, and flourish in their purpose. This has been my amazing second chapter in life.

MY PROVE IT JOURNEY

- *Pain:* I was unconsciously tethering my happiness to success, people, money, and safety.
- *Presence:* I shifted to holding conscious thoughts about what I really wanted to experience (be) in life versus have in life, and I learned to take actions that align and can deliver what I want.
- *Resistance:* I was self-preserving and protecting what I had accumulated—living scared to lose.
- *Release:* I came to understand that some things needed to be lost to free me to have more of what I actually want.
- *Obstacle:* I had a fixed mindset about how things were supposed to be.
- *Observation:* I learned to look for possibilities and stop focusing on the problems—empowering myself to give energy to what I can actually control.
- *Victim:* I relied on others to do and show up as I expected, and when they didn't, I continued to look to them to do and show up as I expected.

- *Valor:* I saw an element of cowardice in me in wanting to stay safe and wanting others to help keep me safe, and when I faced this, I worked to have the courage to not need everything to be so safe.

- *Ego imbalance:* I was encumbered by perceptions, judgments, appearances, and fear, which made me say yes to paths and commitments I should have declined.

- *Ego consciousness:* I learned to be present enough, often enough, in my thoughts and actions to redirect my commitments and create a new pathway to a life that aligns with who I choose to be.

- *Insecurity:* I lived with internal disturbances that I ignored because not ignoring them would have required me to do something about them. But living with them resulted in a duplicitous, unfulfilling existence.

- *Inner peace:* I used valor to show up authentically, honoring and placing my desires and truest self above creating comfort for myself and others.

- *Tip of the iceberg:* I developed the habit of pushing down and pushing away my inner voice that gently alerted me as I drifted further away from myself and beckoned me to take a different direction.

- *Top of the mountain:* I leveled up, embraced a growth mindset, and walked away from the old and toward the new. I dropped my fears and willingly faced a new, bigger mountain that I would have to climb starting from the very bottom.

BRAD'S EPILOGUE

"**MY QUEST HAS TAKEN ME** through the physical, the metaphysical, the delusional—and back. And I have made the most important discovery of my career, the most important discovery of my life: It is only in the mysterious equations of love that any logic or reasons can be found."[1]

This is a quote from one of my favorite movies, *A Beautiful Mind*, starring Russell Crowe. I remember being on the treadmill watching a scene at the end of this movie when Crowe's character, John Nash, was accepting the Nobel Peace Prize. He was talking to a crowd, which included his wife, and expressing his gratitude for her sticking by him through his journey in life. I started crying while I was on the treadmill.

I cried because, in that moment, I was expressing my gratitude to Malitta for sticking with me on my PROVE IT journey. While she stuck with me, she lived her own story of transformation.

What you read in our two stories is the yin and the yang, a Chinese philosophical concept that describes opposite but interconnected forces. Her approach to describing her transformation, yin, is to tell her story with lessons, and my approach, yang, is to give lessons with stories—two different ways of describing the way we both lived and learned from the most challenging time of our lives together.

You will notice we use the same language at times—words like *mindset*, *mindshift*, and *mindful*. Our individual experiences tie back to the concept of yin and yang (irrespective of gender identity). Although we think differently, we are interconnected by the experience we shared and the mindshift we used to understand and recover from it. We both had to PROVE IT—that we believed in the idea that the universe agrees with a made-up mind. In other words, your circumstances, or what you attract to you, have everything to do with how well you understand and manage how your mind works. How the process of being aware of your mindset, changing it through mindshift, and sustaining the change by being mindful is one of the keys to personal and professional success.

Our similar language is no coincidence, and it's another reason I love the movie quote I opened this section with. Malitta and I are both students of metaphysics, the understanding of the meaning beyond the physical. We both came to understand that there was a deeper meaning beyond the experience we shared, and to recover from it, we had to understand that meaning. That understanding, from opposite but interconnected points of view and writing styles, is what we have shared in this book. Hopefully, her yin or my yang, or both, have given you an aha moment or two about yourself, your mindset, and the need (if any) for a mindshift.

Also note the word *love* in the movie quote. That is a very important word and the foundation of our story from my perspective. It is love that kept Malitta with me through *my* journey from the physical to the delusional to the metaphysical. She showed that love through her massive strength to accept me abandoning her in the company, steering the company in and out of the turbulent storm, and then being willing to serve as my mirror to lead me to the self-awareness that started my mindshift.

But love is important for another reason that makes this not just a personal story but a case study that illustrates how loving what you do and pursuing purpose in your life is what keeps you on the pathway to success or what gets you back on that pathway when life or circumstances lead you away from it. I hope this book has done that for you.

MY PROVE IT JOURNEY

- *Pain:* My ego led me (and us) to a state of suffering.
- *Presence:* I journeyed to a state of harmony, where my regrets of the past and fears of the future faded and the opportunities of the present became my focus.
- *Resistance:* I fought against the current so I could steer my life ship where my fixed mindset wanted it to go.
- *Release:* I began to let go and flow with life; my mindset became "mind like water."
- *Obstacle:* I had a mindset of regret, limitation, and fear.
- *Observation:* Being present and conscious allowed me to become an observer. But when I also became attached to nothing, I was willing to move from a path that was not leading me to all the good coming to me.
- *Victim:* I lived in a state of suffering caused by not forgiving my past mistakes.
- *Valor:* I developed bulletproof habits, good habits that helped me generate good thoughts and chase away bad ones.
- *Ego imbalance:* I was controlled by putting myself first and by forces outside me.
- *Ego consciousness:* I (re)found my true self when my journey within led me to an excavation to remove the dirt that had accumulated on me.
- *Insecurity:* I was afraid to stop and decide if I was headed in the right direction; I had a fear mindset.

- *Inner peace:* I pointed toward purpose and attracted the good to me.
- *Tip of the iceberg:* I broke off from what created me, became isolated, and got attacked from all sides.
- *Top of the mountain:* I found my place of transformation, where the forces of uplift created a mountain of support that lifts me up while I stay connected to it.

APPENDIX

PROVE IT MINDSHIFTS JOURNALING GUIDE

Quick Reference Chart for PROVE IT Mindshifts

		Suffering		Stuck		Helpless		Anxious	
Fixed mindset	State of mind								
	Emotional signs	Worried (pain centered)	Defensive (resistant to truth)	Negative (obstacle driven)	Blameful (victim thoughts)	Easily disturbed (ego-imbalanced)	Overly sensitive (insecure)	Distrustful (tip of the iceberg existence)
	Behavior clues	Irritable Regretful Fearful Anxious Envious	Chasing justification Territorial Sensitive Attached to an outcome	Excuse making Naysayer posture Cynicism Low energy Frustration	Outside-in focus Sympathy seeking Lingering hurt Hurt feelings Defensiveness Attached to past	Jealous/comparative Attention and approval seeking Easily bothered Self-conscious	Uncertain Restless Inconsistent Paranoid Overly cautious	Guarded Change averse Hesitant Conflict averse Distant Pessimistic
	Mindshift path →	Move forward in the *present moment* by taking actions that won't re-create regrets of the past or feed worries about the future.		Embrace opportunities to learn new ways of seeing and doing things. Listen more than you speak. Assume others around you have good intentions and can add to the success of the goals you want to achieve.		Look for the role you have played or are playing in the situation you find unpleasant. Consider what you can do differently to create a better outcome for yourself. Accept that the only person you can control is yourself and focus on that.		Reconcile your commitments and decisions with your level of contentment. Figure out what makes you uncomfortable and why. Determine what is within your power to eliminate your discomfort and when will you do it.	
	State of being	Harmonious		Open		Confident		Content	
Open mindset	Mindset qualities	Aware (present)	Flexible (able to release)	Lifelong learner (observant)	Optimistic (victorious/valiant)	Self-confident (ego-conscious)	Receptive (state of inner peace)	Authentic (top of the mountain living)
	Behavior clues	Responsive Accountable Conscientious Approachable	Accepting Positive Resilient Calm Vulnerable	Transparent Good listener Curious Receptive Optimistic	Risk taker Inclusive Positive Forgiving Proactive	Self-aware Self-motivated Nonjudgmental Seeks feedback Collaborative	Emotionally balanced Humble Transparent Trusting Adaptable	Bold Embraces mistakes Respects individuality Purpose-driven

The PROVE IT mindshifts journaling guides on the following pages can help you along the mindshift paths in this chart.

Pain to Presence Mindshift

Pain mindset: Persistent negative thoughts or energy about a situation, person, or experience	Mindshift path: Self-awareness followed by conscious choices and actions	Presence mindset: Staying conscious in present moments, free of fears or thoughts of regret
Typical indicators: • Persistent worry • Sensations of lingering blues or sadness • Longing for people to understand and care about your pain • Being easily disturbed by small and big things • Lingering feelings of anger or resentment • Reactionary posture to protect yourself, at times assuming the worst about what is happening • Convincing yourself you have no choice but to stay in a situation, relationship, or environment Let's journal about the pain: • What is it about the situation, person, or environment that stresses, worries, frustrates, and/or causes you to contort (betray or deny your truest self)? • What is your explanation for staying in what's causing the pain, and what is in the way of your resolving it? • How long have you held your current thoughts and feelings? • What is the likely outcome if you don't take action?	Answer the following questions about the pain around the issue(s) you identified: • What is your desire? • What is your current mindset (do you think more about what is possible or what is limiting/blocking you)? • What factors and driving forces create a disconnection between what you are experiencing and what you desire? Let's explore the pain: • Sit still in the pain for one minute without allowing your mind to race. • Is the strongest feeling of pain generated by something that happened in the past, something that is currently happening, or something you anticipate happening? • How do you want to feel about the person, situation, or environment you're in? Are you willing to move out of the pain? • When have you felt what you want to feel? Make a list of actions you can and will take to create the feelings you want to experience. As you do this, are you self-aware (have a mirror to help you see your part), intellectually aware (understand the facts), and environmentally aware (aware of the impact of what is happening outside you)?	Indicators you have or are making a mindshift: • You're open and receptive to your situation, people, and your environment changing. • Being and remaining self-aware is a priority, and you maintain practices (like identifying trusted sources to serve as mirrors) to support your growth. • You willingly acknowledge when you're wrong and embrace self-accountability. • You allow yourself to be vulnerable about your pain and fears in the situations, with the people, or in the environments involved. • You forgive yourself and others of the past. • You believe positive energy produces optimum outcomes. • You help people you disagree with articulate their point of view to expand your own understanding and bridge differences. • You don't say everything you're thinking. • You pause between your thoughts and your words. • You are conscious about the energy you bring to the situation, person, or experience. Imagine the best version of yourself, and let that vision be your guide in moving away from a mindset of pain and toward being conscious about choices that lift you.

Resistance to Release Mindshift

Resistance mindset: Attachment even when the attachment isn't creating happiness	Mindshift path: Adopting an open mindset to experiencing things differently	Release mindset: Detachment from what once was an acceptance of the flow of life
Typical indicators: • Attachments to what is or what has been • Lingering challenges that eventually increase in intensity • Challenges of a similar nature appearing in different settings and/or with different people • Maintaining half-empty thoughts • Feelings of fear and pessimism • Inviting little to no diversity of thought, experiences, and views in your closest circles • Defensiveness and posturing to convince others of your point of view (argumentative) Let's journal about possible habits of resistance: • What issue have you been dealing with over and over again? Why do think it persists? • How willing are you to consider an opposite point of view? • Are there things people have learned not to debate with you? If so, what are they? • Do you have a go-to statement to back people up from giving you feedback? If so, what is it?	Consider external circumstances in comparison to the desired vision you hold. • What fears do you hold about what might happen if you take a new view or new action about what is or what once was? • Has what you are afraid of ever happened? • If so, what was the outcome, and what did you learn? If not, are you willing to stay in fear and never try? Let's explore resistance: • What are the pros and cons of keeping things as they are? • Can you thrive (optimally expand and grow) with things as they currently are (yes or no)? • What new perspective about what you are resisting can you shift to today? What cons exist about this perspective? • What can you do to counter the impact of the cons? • Number your answers to the question above starting with 1 as most difficult and continuing until you get through your list. • Starting with the highest number (least difficult), decide on a date to take the first step to making it happen. If something is too difficult to do alone, stop and get help from someone you trust or a professional trained in the area (or both).	Indicators you have or are making a mindshift: • You've adopted a "mind like water" posture, embracing changes with an open mind and balanced emotions. • You set goals and desires but you're able to remain detached from expectations. • You design more than one path to your goals. • You seek input from people who don't think or see things as you do. • You honor change as part of life. • You focus on co-creating versus controlling. • You listen to understand others' points of view and no longer find yourself thinking of answers before others finish speaking. • You are not defensive or irritated by ideas and perspectives that don't align with what you envisioned. • You have new perspectives about things you once felt strongly about. • Differences no longer disturb you. Thinking is an action. Once we think a thought, we have taken a step that moves us in a direction that aligns with that thought. Before allowing your mind to build on a thought, pause and decide if the action of that thought will move you forward, keep you stuck, or move you backward.

Appendix: PROVE IT Mindshifts Journaling Guide 205

Obstacles to Observation Mindshift

Obstacle mindset: A tendency to focus on problems and what could go wrong	Mindshift path: Embracing challenges as opportunities	Observation mindset: Objectively observing situations before participating and responding
Typical indicators: • Gravitates to what is wrong • Generates thoughts and ideas rooted in a focus on problems • Feeling like there are no good answers • Talking over others when they attempt to point out the positive • Needing your view to be right and rejecting other possibilities before giving them careful consideration • Focusing on right now more than the longer term • Afraid to ask questions that might negate your feelings • Believing things are happening outside your control • Reactive rather than proactive • Allowing challenges to escalate, not pivoting and taking timely action to create better outcomes Let's journal about the obstacle(s): • Describe the threat posed by the obstacle(s). • If you allow the obstacle(s) to remain, what is the longer-term benefit or loss? • Which of the two responses above (the benefit or loss) is most desired? Which will you wish you had chosen six months or a year from now? • List resources that can help you navigate the better answer.	Imagine that you hate roller coasters and you're watching yourself as an observer and not the participant as you take a ride on one. • What do you observe yourself thinking as the ride approaches the top of the slope? • What feelings are your thoughts generating—fear, anxiety, paralysis, etc.? • When you get safely to the end of the slope, do you think your thoughts were correct and the feelings were valid? As an observer, would you now choose to have different thoughts and feelings as you face the second slope? Let's explore obstacles: • Look at the obstacle(s) you wrote about in your journal as an observer (detaching from feelings of fear, paralysis, etc.) and imagine you are advising someone else about the obstacle(s). • On a scale of 1 to 10 (with 10 being the most important), rank each obstacle in terms of how significant it is that the person you are advising (you) do something about it. • List the obstacles with the highest scores first. If you have only one obstacle on your list, address that one. If any have the same score, prioritize the one that, if solved, makes some of the other obstacles below it go away. • For the highest obstacle on the list, create a list of actions you can take to address and resolve it so that it no longer triggers negative thoughts and fears.	Indicators you have or are making a mindshift: • You've begun to self-coach using positive thoughts driven by facts, not emotions—asking yourself, "What would I advise someone else?" • You've shifted from a posture of reacting to a practice of pausing, observing, and seeking outside input from unbiased sources before responding. • You remember that 95 percent of what is feared never happens, and when it does, it isn't typically as bad as imagined. • You give yourself permission to change your mind (your thoughts) and courageously shift when a shift is needed. • You are able to step back and look at what is happening like you are not in it. • You prioritize self-awareness—you want to know what your mirrors see. • You point the finger at yourself first for solutions. • You show empathy and compassion toward others without compromising what is needed to overcome obstacles. Obstacles are things we accept as challenges but not as barriers. Before giving something or someone the power to block, explore the truth about its significance. Then observe it, define it, and identify doable strategies and actions to remove it.

Victim to Valor Mindshift

Victim mindset: Recurring thoughts about what happened or was done to you	Mindshift path: Self-empowerment and awareness in present experiences	Valor mindset: Acceptance without blame or resentment
Typical indicators: - Feeling used or taken advantage of by others - Recurring thoughts that circumstances exist because of others - A resistance to owning options to reverse the impact of negative experiences - Hearing the bully's voice louder than the ally's—repeating narratives that keep unwanted experiences alive - Seeking opportunities to share and recount disappointment - Surrounding yourself with sympathizers who allow and maybe even encourage negative and unproductive thoughts while avoiding people who challenge you to create a new truth - Using tactics (like getting upset) to keep others from telling you the truth Let's journal about victimhood: - Fill in the blank, "If _____ had (or had not) happened, I would be _____." - What role is this thought playing in your life (when and how often does it come to mind)? - What could help remove the thought? - Who and what could help you move past the pain, narrative, and tendency to keep it alive (therapist, a mentor, etc.)?	Think about the situation or relationship that triggers victim-nature thoughts and feelings. - In what ways would things be different had the experience not happened? - In what ways is it showing up today? - Is there another possible perspective to your view? - Are you willing to create a new thought (narrative) and respond to the experience differently? Let's explore *thinking* like a victim: - Describe a situation where you feel you were or are being treated unfairly. - Do you believe you were (or are) the intended or unintended recipient of the harm? - If you believe you were the intended target, is it possible to discuss the experience with those who created it to share the impact on you and gain their perspective? - If you believe you were the unintended target, what would be the impact of shifting your narrative to one that reminds you it was unintentional? - Are you willing to let the experience go? If yes, write down a mantra that will help shift you away from the thought pattern. If not, consider seeking outside support. *Example mantra: To not be a victim, I must move forward and not back. That is why the windshield is larger than the rearview mirror.*	Indicators you have or are making a mindshift: - You're willing to brave the step of taking responsibility for creating a new reality. - Your desire to live free of the experiences is stronger than your desire for justice or justification for holding on to anger or disappointment. - You've released energy-draining narratives and replaced them with energy-lifting thoughts. - You embrace that people do the best they can based on the stage of enlightenment and awareness they are in at any given time. - You no longer protect the pain by teaching others to not share perspectives you used to not want to hear. - You don't feel a need to talk about it or seek validation and don't need others to dislike the person or people who caused the situation. - You can operate from a posture of trust. - You accept that growth can come from negative experiences. Fear can be a factor. Sometimes it is easier to place the responsibility for unwanted circumstances outside of us than it is to face what we might have to do to get beyond them. (This is an area where professional support and guidance is strongly encouraged.)

Note: These strategies are not written to address trauma.

Appendix: PROVE IT Mindshifts Journaling Guide 207

Ego Imbalanced to Ego Aware Mindshift

Ego imbalanced mindset: Patterns of self-inflating or self-deflating thoughts and actions	Mindshift path: Life purpose and impact matter more than recognition or insecurities	Ego aware mindset: A conscious shift away from self-importance or self-sabotage
Typical indicators: • Needing things to be about you and your needs or too readily placing your priorities on a back burner • Wanting complete control or too easily deferring your control • Needing to be right or giving in on your opinion too easily, even when you know it is the right one • Consistently talking more than you listen or not speaking up when you should • Consistently wanting to brag about yourself and show what you're doing or never feeling comfortable promoting yourself • Being argumentative to the point that being right is the objective or bowing out of discussions prematurely because you fear being wrong • Consistent desire to be the center of attention or consistent efforts to avoid the spotlight • Frequent feelings of jealousy or a habit of comparing yourself to others Let's journal about the imbalanced ego: • Generally, when interacting with others, how often do you have thoughts of comparison, thoughts about what you think they are thinking of you, or thoughts of superiority or inferiority? • How do you think these thoughts affect your behavior? • Write down the parts of your ego (your identity) that you like and dislike.	Consciously develop your ego (you have one). • How do you want your ego to show up? • How do you think others (your mirrors) see it showing up? • In what situations or with whom could there be a difference between what you want your ego to be and what others might be experiencing? • What might be driving the difference between the two? Let's explore the imbalanced ego: • When you think about your achievements, using a scale of 1 to 5, with 5 being the most important, how important is it that others know about your achievements? • How quickly do you typically recover from failures, embarrassment, or feelings of inadequacy—somewhat immediately, over time, or never (meaning the bully mind keeps the memory alive through triggers)? • Is there anything about the responses to the two questions above you would like to change? If so, what can you begin to do today to counter them? If there is nothing you want to change, write out what you like and would like to expand. • List situations you've noticed that generate ego-imbalanced behaviors. In what ways can you be more conscious and exhibit a more balanced ego? • Consider writing these balanced-ego behaviors in a journal every morning. Writing them is more effective than just reading them. Consider the My Morning BAGELS journaling described in chapter 8.	Indicators you have or are making a mindshift: • You don't have to be "the one" to always get the credit or "the one" to make all the sacrifices. • An attachment to being out in the front or staying in the background doesn't drive how you show up. • Applause and judgment are no longer as important as the impact of living within your purpose. • You share your input without overthinking or calculating how it will be viewed. • You have an open mind, want others to succeed while you also succeed, and pursue balance in relationships. • You accept being wrong or failing at something as an opportunity for growth. • You care more about living authentically than pleasing and being what you think others think you are or should be. A balanced-ego mindset is rooted in self-awareness and vulnerability. When we are aware of the outside forces that create an imbalance of fears, self-esteem, and concerns about relevance, significance, and acceptance, we can control them.

Insecurity to Inner Peace Mindshift

Insecurity mindset: Feeling guarded, defensive, fearful, and/or alone	Mindshift path: Embracing and celebrating your individuality/authenticity	Inner peace mindset: Balance of external commitments with inner contentment
Typical indicators: • Needing constant reassurance and affirmation • Placing more value on what other people think of you than what you think of yourself • Second-guessing yourself long after conversations have ended • Reading meaning into what people have said to you without verifying your assumptions • Allowing past mistakes to overpower current experiences • Uncomfortable or agitated if people disagree with you openly in front of others • Protective of your territory and areas of knowledge • Would rather have people not tell you the truth to avoid being vulnerable • Overly reliant on title, position, or having control Let's journal about insecurity: • In what situations or with whom does being vulnerable make you uncomfortable? • When you are in those situations, what feels like a threat? • List situations when (and people with whom) being vulnerable feels safe. • List anything about your mindset that contributes to the difference between feeling a threat and feeling safe. (See the glossary for the definition of mindset.)	Embrace, celebrate, and elevate your individuality. • Do you give deference to expectations from external sources above your authenticity and individuality? • When, with whom, or in what situations have you given yourself permission to contort? • Are there situations in which or people with whom you feel unheard, unseen, or not known? What part do you play in this dynamic? Let's explore insecurity: • What is your definition of contorting and how do you feel when you contort? • List situations when you tend to cross the line of compromise into a zone of contortion. • What do you tell yourself when you cross this line? • Is there any part of you that you regret neglecting when you do this? • What parts of you do you feel you neglect or lose when you do this? • What would happen if you stopped contorting in these situations? • Consider the situations and people that don't require you to contort. Is there a way to replicate those dynamics in situations and with the people when you contort? (Remember the difference between compromising and contorting.)	Indicators you have or are making a mindshift: • You are not easily disturbed by things outside your control. • You have conscious practices that keep you connected with your authenticity. • You pause before speaking and committing (you resist responding out of habit and expectation). • You leave situations and conversations in peace without overthinking them. • You embrace being wrong as an opportunity to learn. • You are receptive to constructive feedback. • You make fewer excuses about who and how you are. • You commit to self-growth and inner expression. • You are conscious of the difference between having an opinion and being judgmental. • You seek and build authentic relationships. • You prefer being at peace over being popular. Living in insecurity causes internal stress and conflict. It is a robber of joy. External forces can pressure you to give yourself away until you get to a point of struggle to create happiness. Inner peace comes as you find ways to honor and shine your unique energy and gifts in natural ways from within you, not outside you.

Tip of the Iceberg to Top of the Mountain Mindshift

Tip of the iceberg mindset: Showing and giving the world only what appears to fit	Mindshift path: Honoring what is within you and what awaits you	Top of the mountain mindset: Reconnection to purpose for happiness
Typical indicators: • Recurring feelings of disconnection or isolation • Recurring thoughts that aren't fully aligned with what is externally shared • Change avoidance; tethering to structure and routines • Hesitancy to make decisions without committee input • Disturbed by people who are not predictable • Reliance on having crafted and careful responses • Routinely appropriate, orderly, and predictable • External reputation is a high priority • Noticeable gaps between work and home persona • Fears of rejection • Willing to adapt to the audience of the moment • Needing to have control to feel safe Let's journal about being an iceberg: • In what situations do you mostly only show part of who you really are? • What is your motivation (reason) for doing this, and do you feel it is valid? Why or why not? • What would happen if you stopped sharing only the parts of you that feel safe to share? • List the parts of you the world is not experiencing—the unique parts of you that are typically suppressed.	Originality is a superpower. Maximize the experience of your magnificence. • How often do you have thoughts and ideas you stifle because you fear judgment, rejection, or conflict? • Do you fear you'll lose the life you have if you choose to live out loud as your truest, most authentic self? Let's explore iceberg living: • Make a list of recurring inner thoughts you have about who you are, your gifts, or your desires in life that you suppress and don't share. • Write out exactly what you envision happening if you share and give life to the most pressing ones. • Does what you envision offer a more beneficial and fulfilling life in the long run? Why or why not? • If the answer above is yes, write out a strategy and actions to begin to share and live in alignment with your truth. (Remember, the plan doesn't have to be an overnight shift.) If the answer to the previous question is no, explain to yourself in detail why it is better to stay as you are, and then decide if your explanation is acceptable. Revisit this explanation to yourself until you are comfortable it is the right answer.	Indicators you have or are making a mindshift: • You understand that heeding your higher calling can lift your life and the lives of others. • You have shifted from a posture of self-preservation to purpose. • You understand that your connection to what is outside you is better when it is driven by what is inside you (not the other way around). • You operate to do good and not just receive good. • You are intentional about surrounding yourself with others who are purpose-driven. • You are more concerned about and define your value based on who you are being, not what you are doing. • You view and honor money as energy and consciously circulate it to promote good energy for yourself and others. • You pursue but don't compete, understanding that there is no one to compete with to achieve internal contentment. Reaching your own mountaintop experiences is a decision. It might require abandoning the safety of predictable paths and roads, or perhaps it's simply a shift in how you view and label your life. In either case, the most important block or flow to getting there is you.

NOTES

Chapter 3

1. Brené Brown, "The Power of Vulnerability," TEDxHouston, June 2010, https://www.ted.com/talks/brene_brown_the_power_of_vulnerability?subtitle=en.
2. Spencer Johnson, *Who Moved My Cheese?* (G. P. Putnam's Sons, 1998), 60.

Chapter 4

1. Esther and Jerry Hicks, *Ask and It Is Given* (Hay House, 2004), 49.
2. Michael A. Singer, *The Untethered Soul: The Journey Beyond Yourself* (New Harbinger, 2007).
3. Nelson Mandela, *Long Walk to Freedom* (Little, Brown, 2008), Kindle loc. 43.
4. See, for example, Joyce Meyer, "Embracing Life Beyond Abuse Through Faith," Joyce Meyer Ministries, accessed October 23, 2024, https://joycemeyer.org/Grow-Your-Faith/Articles/Life-Beyond-Abuse.

Chapter 5

1. *Oxford English Dictionary*, s.v. "ego," accessed October 4, 2024, https://www.oed.com/dictionary/ego_n?tab=factsheet#5779196.
2. Kenneth Klonsky, "Going the Distance," *The Sun*, August 2023, https://www.thesunmagazine.org/articles/22547-going-the-distance.

Part II

1. Ryan Holiday, *Ego Is the Enemy* (Portfolio, 2016).

Chapter 8

1. Ryan Holiday, *Ego Is the Enemy* (Portfolio, 2016).
2. Carol S. Dweck, *Mindset: The New Psychology of Success* (Ballantine Books, 2007).
3. Deepak Chopra, *The Seven Spiritual Laws of Success: A Pocket Guidebook to Fulfilling Your Dreams* (Amber-Allen, 2015), 19.

Chapter 9

1. Tasha Eurich, *Insight* (Crown Currency, 2017).
2. See, for example, Ellie Lisitsa, "The Four Horsemen: Criticism, Contempt, Defensiveness, and Stonewalling," Gottman Institute, October 15, 2024, https://www.gottman.com/blog/the-four-horsemen-recognizing-criticism-contempt-defensiveness-and-stonewalling.

3. See, for example, Simon Young, "How to Increase Serotonin in the Human Brain Without Drugs," *Journal of Psychiatry and Neuroscience* 32, no. 6 (2007): 394–399.

Chapter 10

1. See, for example, John A. Bargh and Ezequiel Morsella, "The Unconscious Mind," *Perspectives on Psychological Science* 3, no. 1 (2008), https://pmc.ncbi.nlm.nih.gov/articles/PMC2440575/.
2. Avinash De Sousa, "Freudian Theory and Consciousness: A Conceptual Analysis," *Mens Sana Monographs* 9, no. 1 (2011): 210–217.
3. Paul Hasselbeck, "The Law of Mind Action," Unity, accessed October 7, 2024, https://www.unity.org/article/law-mind-action.
4. Susan Jeffers, *Feel the Fear . . . and Do It Anyway* (Ballantine Books, 2007), 182–184.

Chapter 11

1. Marianne Williamson, *A Return to Love: Reflections on the Principles of "A Course in Miracles"* (HarperOne, 1996).

Chapter 12

1. Emily McDowell (@emilyonlife), Instagram post, February 15, 2019, https://www.instagram.com/p/Bt61ebll9IV.
2. Wayne Dyer, *You'll See It When You Believe It* (William Morrow, 2001), 69.
3. Charles Fillmore, *The Twelve Powers of Man* (Unity School of Christianity, 1930).
4. Deepak Chopra, *The Seven Spiritual Laws of Success: A Pocket Guidebook to Fulfilling Your Dreams* (Amber-Allen, 2015).

Malitta's Epilogue

1. *Online Entomology Dictionary*, s.v. "enjoyment," accessed November 18, 2024, https://www.etymonline.com/word/enjoyment#etymonline_v_32570.
2. *Online Entomology Dictionary*, s.v. "joy," accessed October 7, 2024, https://www.etymonline.com/word/joy.
3. Dictionary.com, s.v. "joy," accessed October 7, 2024, https://www.dictionary.com/browse/joy.

Brad's Epilogue

1. *A Beautiful Mind*, dir. Ron Howard (Universal Pictures, 2001).

GLOSSARY

Awareness. The state of being conscious or mindful; a key element in personal growth and transformation and decision-making. *See also* Environmental awareness; Intellectual awareness; Self-awareness.

Conscious mind. The part of the mind that is actively aware of and focused on thoughts, feelings, and experiences in the present moment. This is the part of the mind that governs how we intentionally behave in the moment.

Ego. A person's sense of self-esteem or pride. It can describe an inflated sense of self-worth, leading to arrogance; a healthy self-esteem that helps one navigate life confidently; or an underactivated ego that can lead to a poor self-image that causes one to be taken advantage of or not stand up for themselves. The ego affects decision-making. *See also* Id; Superego.

Environmental awareness. Being conscious of what exists and is true outside and around us. This helps us balance the internal with the external before moving in a certain direction.

Fear. An emotional response to a perceived threat of danger. This alerts us to fight, flee, or freeze. At a healthy level, it makes us cautious and leads to actions that can protect us. At unhealthy levels, it can lead to stress, anxiety, inaction, or other behaviors that negatively affect our peace of mind and happiness. Sometimes used as an acronym for "false evidence appearing real," which suggests that most of what we fear at unhealthy levels never happens.

Four Horsemen. A term, coined by psychologist Dr. John Gottman, to describe four destructive behaviors in relationships. These behaviors are as follows. (1) *Contempt:* Possibly the most damaging of the horsemen, this is when an individual is condescending to another and shows no respect. It often comes in the form of name-calling, threats, or insults. A person who engages in contempt puts the other person down, expresses superiority (maybe even by mocking the other person), and in many ways declares war. (2) *Criticism:* This is blaming the other person by expressing that there is something wrong with them or who they are—that is, attacking their character or flaws. Complaining about the way someone is *behaving* can be effective, but criticizing who they *are* as a person can be damaging and is rarely productive. (3) *Defensiveness:* This is when we feel personally attacked and take position to protect ourselves. The "attack" can be as simple as someone telling us to remember to take out the trash. The defense we give back can ward off the perceived attack and effectively keep something true about us or our behavior hidden from sight (for instance, perhaps the real problem is we resent being told when and what to do). The goal is to make the other person stand down and back off. (4) *Stonewalling:* This is when we disengage because we feel flooded by the feedback we receive from someone else. The disengagement sends the message that either we are not listening or we are ignoring the feedback. This can incite the other person and intensify their attack.

Gaslighting. Responding to criticism by redirecting the person who is giving the feedback in ways that cause them to question their memory or perception. Common phrases include "You're imagining things" or "You're overreacting." The impact on the other person can be loss of self-esteem and increased self-doubt.

Higher power. A force greater than individual, human power that is typically viewed as transcendent, divine, or supreme. God (or the superior being of one's belief system), the universe, nature, the indwelling spirit of individuals, the cosmos, and other forces are examples of higher powers.

Higher self. The transcendent part of an individual that is the deeper more enlightened version of themselves connected to the higher external power of their beliefs.

Id. Our primitive (internal) impulse thinking and instincts for survival and pleasure.

Inbound. A mindset of going inward, within oneself, to a place of origin, to identify, understand, and gain an awareness of the self that drives thoughts, feelings, decisions, and desires; a journey of self-excavation to eliminate sabotaging blind spots and personal barriers.

Intellectual awareness. The ability to analyze, comprehend, and assess knowledge and situations. This helps us see the big picture so we can connect the dots between what is required and what affects things we want or don't want.

Leadership. An ability to guide and inspire others toward a common vision that is significantly influenced by life experiences, self-awareness, passion, and empathy for others.

Life. The journey of loving, experiencing, growing, and sharing our individuality with others while learning and demonstrating why we are here.

Light blockers. Emotions, feelings, and thoughts that hinder or reduce the ability to be present, conscious, and free from negativity. Examples include emotional triggers, personality blind spots, rigid mindsets, ego, fear, doubt, and shame.

Love. An emotion rooted in compassion and deep care for someone or something; feelings and actions of respect, understanding, and acceptance that enhance the sense of purpose in life.

Metaphysics. The foundation for the New Thought movement, which studies the underlying truths of life that go beyond the physical realm. Its philosophy is a practical tool for understanding and applying universal laws to create a more peaceful, fulfilling, and harmonious existence.

Mindful. Being present when decisions, thoughts, and behaviors are in action and generated from the conscious mind; an antidote to unconscious thinking and living, negating automatic responses that can result in recurring unwanted experiences.

Mindset. The attitudes, beliefs, and ways of thinking that affect the lens through which we process information and respond to experiences. Although a mindset can exist about any subject or experience, psychologist Carol Dweck identified two broad types of mindsets: *fixed mindset*, a belief that a person's abilities, intelligence, limitations, and talents cannot change, and *growth mindset*, a belief that a person's abilities, intelligence, potential, and talents can be developed.

Mindset freedom. A way of thinking that is absent of limiting beliefs and mental patterns that block us from achieving peace, harmony, happiness, joy, and success; a commitment to maintaining an open mind.

Mindshift. A transformative change in the way a person thinks, perceives, or approaches a situation, belief, or challenge, to create better and more sustainable experiences and outcomes; a fundamental shift in mindset; a break away from old ways of thinking.

Mirror. A person committed to giving honest and truthful feedback to another for the purpose of making that person more self-aware and conscious of their blind spots.

Self-awareness. The ability to recognize and understand your thoughts, feelings, and behaviors, as well as how they affect the people around you; a trait that helps us not lie to ourselves about our blind spots and accept responsibility for managing our light blockers.

Subconscious mind. The part of the mind that operates automatically based on memories, beliefs, patterns, and feelings related to what has been seen, done, or experienced in the past. Many daily habits reside here. It is important to note that most subconscious thoughts are not repressed but instead are stored just below conscious awareness and can become accessible (sometimes quickly) through introspection, reflection, or specific techniques like mindfulness or therapy.

Superego. Where more conscious thoughts are generated to align with values in society (external) so we can create experiences of reward (or punishment).

Unconscious mind. The part of the mind that is outside conscious awareness; the storehouse of thoughts, memories, feelings, desires, and experiences that are repressed or buried. The contents of the unconscious mind can include painful, embarrassing, or unpleasant memories and feelings that affect behavior and generate automatic responses to certain triggers experienced in day-to-day interactions.

Universe. The system and sum of everything that exists, creating an interconnectedness of all things material and immaterial, such as consciousness, energy, ideas, and spiritual dimensions. It is not limited to the observable or measurable but includes potential realities and possibilities. All the components within it work together to generate the outcomes and experiences that happen in life.

Yang. Originates from Chinese philosophy and represents qualities such as strength, assertiveness, and control.

Yin. Originates from Chinese philosophy and represents qualities such as sensitivity, intuition, and nurturing.

ABOUT THE AUTHORS

MALITTA SEAMON is a business strategist, a coach, an author, a speaker, and an adviser to executives and leaders. She cofounded Inbound Leadership (www.inboundleadership.com), an organization dedicated to strengthening and supporting leaders by creating safe spaces for them to reflect, be vulnerable, and grow (her passion). Inbound Leadership is committed to the whole being of leaders, not just their technical aptitude. The organization supports mental, physical, and energy well-being through practical mindful habits. Malitta and Inbound Leadership's vision is a world of mindful leaders. Malitta is a certified executive coach, certified relationship coach, certified nutritionist, and trained breathwork practitioner.

BRAD SEAMON is an executive in the health care industry (his passion), where he works to merge the interests and needs of the community with the services and priorities of the health care system he works with. He has dedicated most of his career to helping leaders grow, promote, and develop their organizations and programs on local, national, and international levels. He is a consultant and board member of Malitta's organization, Inbound Leadership, where he serves as a content contributor, retreat facilitator, and speaker. Brad is a certified public accountant, certified professional coach, and certified DISC and emotional intelligence coach.

Malitta and Brad have been married for thirty-seven years and reside in Maryland. They have two sons, Brad Jr. and Chad; a daughter-in-law, Danielle; and two granddaughters, Parker and Kendall.

INBOUND LEADERSHIP

Creating communities of inbound leaders

Inbound leadership: The act of traveling inward, to a place of origin, to gain a better understanding and awareness of the self for the purpose of reemerging with more authenticity; a journey of excavation to eliminate blind spots and personal barriers for greater leadership impact and rebooting mindsets to experience better success and joy.

MINDSET AWARENESS	MINDSHIFT ENGAGEMENT	MINDFUL PRACTICES
Attitudes, beliefs, and ways of thinking that affect the lens through which information and experiences are processed. The *driving force of personal responses* that is typically rooted in a fixed perspective of limitations or a growth perspective that embraces change. A major influence on success and happiness.	A *transformational change* in the way a person thinks about, perceives, or approaches a situation, belief, or challenge, to create better and more sustainable experiences and outcomes. A fundamental shift in mindset; a break away from old ways of thinking and an embrace of new possibilities to expand personal growth.	Being present when decisions, thoughts, and behaviors are in action and generated *from the conscious mind*; an antidote to unconscious thinking and living, negating automatic responses that can result in recurring and unwanted experiences. Consciously focused on here and now, void of past regrets or future fears.

Personal transformation creates collective transformation.

The Inbound Leadership purpose: Inbound Leadership (IL) exists to expand self-awareness and provide continuous learning experiences for CEOs and leaders in safe, supportive spaces. We know firsthand the impact effective (and ineffective) leadership can have, not only on organizational culture and environment but also on local, national, and global communities. Our mission is to advance a movement for leaders to understand the power of mindset, the importance of mindshifting, and the benefits of leading mindfully.

INFO@INBOUNDLEADERSHIP.COM
WWW.INBOUNDLEADERSHIP.COM

www.ingramcontent.com/pod-product-compliance
Lightning Source LLC
Chambersburg PA
CBHW060520080526
44586CB00012B/557